Twayne's United States Authors Series

Sylvia E. Bowman, *Editor*

INDIANA UNIVERSITY

S. N. Behrman

TUSAS 256

Photo by Lotte Jacobi courtesy of Little Brown and Company

S. N. Behrman

S. N. BEHRMAN

By KENNETH T. REED

Miami University

TWAYNE PUBLISHERS

A DIVISION OF G. K. HALL & CO., BOSTON

Library of Congress Cataloging in Publication Data

Reed, Kenneth T
  S. N. Behrman.

  (Twayne's United States authors series)
  Bibliography: pp. 141–46.
  Includes index.
  1. Behrman, Samuel Nathan, 1893–1973.
PS3503.E37Z85   812'.5'2 [B]   75-2085
ISBN 0-8057-7154-9

FOR BILLY, LIZA AND ANNE

Contents

About the Author

Kenneth T. Reed completed his undergraduate studies in literature at Miami University (Ohio). In 1961 he received the M.A. degree with emphasis in twentieth century literature from the University of Iowa. He completed the Ph.D. degree in American literature at the University of Kentucky in 1968. Since that time he has been a member of the English faculty at Miami University. He currently holds the rank of Associate Professor.

Professor Reed has written extensively for scholarly journals on such writers as Harriet Beecher Stowe, Richard Wright, Mark Twain, Stephen Crane, F. Scott Fitzgerald, Emily Dickinson, William Dean Howells, and Washington Irving. His articles, notes, and reviews have been published in *Literature and Psychology, Poe Studies, American Notes & Queries, Studies in Black Literature, The American Transcendental Quarterly,* the *CLA Journal,* and the *Fitzgerald/Hemingway Annual.*

Preface

My approach to Samuel Nathaniel Behrman in this book is both critical and biographical, for I have found that any discussion of Behrman the writer is virtually impossible without taking into account some aspects of the man. Another reason I have been more biography-conscious than I am accustomed to being is that Behrman led a very private kind of life, and the things that are known about him are, at best, fragmentary. My first impulse when I prepared to write, therefore, was to include a biographical chapter that was both factual and coherent.

I discovered in my research that there was no comprehensive treatment of Behrman's considerable number of plays and essays except that in an unpublished doctoral dissertation by Lewis Williams Heniford at Stanford University in 1964. Among the numerous other articles and reviews written over the years about Behrman and his work, I found little continuity. After I had read and reread the Behrman plays and essays a number of times, my critical estimation took an unexpected turn, for I became convinced that, although he had become famous as a playwright, his true literary gift was far less in the writing of plays than in the writing of essays. This realization, more than any other, was the one that has given this book its shape. If the amount of space devoted to the plays seems disproportionately great, it is because of Behrman's more familiar reputation as a playwright.

With this much decided, I attempted to trace the development of Behrman's main thematic concerns such as money, matrimony, success, and the need for toleration. Because Behrman's point of view changed rather little over the years, I gradually became aware of what to look for in his writing; and I have endeavored to call these things to the attention of the reader. I have devoted comparatively little space to other matters, such as the work of Behrman's playwriting contemporaries and his personal and literary relationships with them.

In general, the organization of this study tends to follow the ebb and flow of Behrman's career as writer. After the biographical chapter, I concentrate on Behrman's literary apprenticeship when he formed some of the opinions that were to remain with him. I recognized that this apprenticeship ended, for the most part, with his first important theatrical success, *The Second Man*, in 1927. In chapter 3 ("The Prime Years"), I evaluate seven significant plays that appeared on Broadway between 1927 and 1936. Chapter 4 considers the lesser plays, those that were produced from 1937 to 1964. Chapter 5 discusses Behrman's achievement in nondramatic literature where, as I have indicated, most of his best work is to be found. "The Major Themes" (chapter 6) explains itself, and chapter 7 ("Matters of Technique") is an analysis of the Behrman style and some of the literary forces that helped to create it. The closing chapter is a general assessment of the man as writer.

Books such as this are never written single-handedly, and this particular effort could not have been completed without the aid of a number of people. Mr. S. N. Behrman was especially kind and helpful through the letters he was good enough to send me and through an afternoon interview in his New York apartment, which he granted me in spite of his deteriorating health. Even a telephone conversation with him, as a reporter for *The New Yorker* said recently, was a delightful experience. His personal secretaries, first Mrs. Grace Wherry and later his niece Mrs. Anne Grossman, have corresponded with me on many occasions, and they have unfailingly answered my questions with accuracy and dispatch. Lewis Williams Heniford of Carmel, California, helped me immeasurably by making available to me his meticulously ordered notes on Behrman which he had used in the preparation of his doctoral dissertation.

Other persons were generous in other ways. Hiram J. Behrman of New York City supplied me with some necessary family information. Harley P. Holden of the Harvard University Library was able to enlighten me about some aspects of Behrman's years at Harvard. Marion Henderson of the Clark University Library supplied me with some valuable specimens of Behrman's early writing at Clark College. W. Danforth Hayes, librarian at the *Worcester Telegram & Gazette*, turned up some important biographical leads from his files, as did Gerard T. Corcoran, registrar at Clark University.

Several other persons have been extraordinarily generous with help and encouragement. Miami University afforded me a summer research appointment and other forms of financial aid as well. To Dean Spiro Peterson of the Graduate School I am thankful for sustained interest as well as some bibliographical contributions. Mr. Leland Dutton and Ms. Joan Ten Hoor, two especially capable librarians, spent hours locating materials I had thought inaccessible. Professor Homer Abegglen, with his encyclopedic knowledge of the theater, aided me with bibliographical advice before I began writing and with expert criticism after I had completed the first of many drafts. No less valuable was the painstaking attention to style given the manuscript by my good friend Mrs. Dorothy Beeler. My severest taskmaster, however, was Dr. Sylvia Bowman, without whose vast editorial experience this book would never have gone to press. Finally, I must not omit the credit to my wife for the encouragement I received when I most needed it. All of these persons, and others, have gone far out of their way for my sake. Whatever imperfections are to be found within the covers of this volume are accountable only to me.

K. T. REED

Miami University
Hamilton, Ohio

Acknowledgments

The author is grateful for permissions to reprint from the published works of S. N. Behrman as authorized by the following parties: to Stein and Day Publishers, permission to quote from *The Suspended Drawing Room*, Copyright 1939, 1940, 1944, 1945, 1946, 1947, 1965 by S. N. Behrman; to Samuel French, Inc., permission to quote from *Meteor*, Copyright 1925, 1927, 1928, 1930, 1934 by S. N. Behrman, and from *I Know My Love*, Copyright 1947 (under title *Auprès de Ma Blonde*) by Editions Jean Michel, Copyright 1949 by S. N. Behrman, Copyright 1952 (Acting Edition) by S. N. Behrman. Copies of these plays, in individual paperback acting editions, are available from Samuel French, Inc., 25 W. 45th St., New York, N.Y. 10036, or 7623 Sunset Blvd., Hollywood, Calif. 90046, or in Canada, Samuel French (Canada) Ltd., 26 Grenville St., Toronto 5, Canada; to Little, Brown and Company, permission to quote from *People in a Diary: A Memoir*, Copyright 1972 by S. N. Behrman; to Random House, Inc., permission to quote from *The Worcester Account*, Copyright 1954 by S. N. Behrman, from *Portrait of Max: An Intimate Memoir of Sir Max Beerbohm*, Copyright 1960 by S. N. Behrman; from *Duveen*, Copyright 1952 by S. N. Behrman; from *Lord Pengo*, Copyright 1963 by S. N. Behrman; from *But for Whom Charlie*, Copyright 1964 by S. N. Behrman; from *The Cold Wind and the Warm*, Copyright 1959 by S. N. Behrman; from *4 Plays by S. N. Behrman*, Copyright 1925, 1932, 1934, 1935, 1936, 1952 by S. N. Behrman; from *Fanny*, Copyright 1954 by S. N. Behrman; to Brandt & Brandt, permission to quote from *The Pirate*, Copyright 1943, 1971 by S. N. Behrman; from *Wine of Choice*, Copyright 1943, 1971 by S. N. Behrman; from *The Talley Method*, Copyright 1941, 1969 by S. N. Behrman; from *Brief Moment*, Copyright 1931, 1959 by S. N. Behrman; from *Dunnigan's Daughter*, Copyright 1945 as an unpublished play by S. N. Behrman and Copyright 1946

Chronology

1893 Samuel Nathaniel Behrman born in Worcester, Massachusetts, on approximately June 9, the third child of Joseph and Zelda (Feingold) Behrman. Their first two children, Hiram and Morris, were born in Europe.

1899 Attends Providence Street School in Worcester.

1902 Hears a campaign speech by Eugene V. Debs.

1904 Sees his first play, *Devil's Island*, in the company of friend Daniel Asher.

1907 Enters Classical High School in Worcester.

1908 Begins lifelong interest in literature.

1909 Hears Sigmund Freud lecture at Clark College.

1911 Tours with the Poli vaudeville circuit performing in a skit of his own making. Health fails; returns to Worcester.

1912 Enters Clark College in Worcester as a special student. Father dies in October. Brothers both working in New York.

1913 Becomes an assistant to the Board of Publications at Clark. Enters a public speaking contest; plays a role in Henrik Ibsen's *An Enemy of the People*. Suspended from Clark for failure to attend physical education classes. Enrolls in Harvard Summer School.

1914 Reenters Clark College. Takes part in Menorah Society activities, in theater presentations, and in the Socialist Club. Majors in English and compiles a good record but is suspended from Clark again for not attending physical education classes. Submits a play to George Pierce Baker and transfers to Harvard late in the summer.

1915 Studies English composition with Charles Townsend Copeland at Harvard. Sells his first story, "La Vie Parisienne," for fifteen dollars.

1916 Enrolls in Baker's English 47 playwriting course. Graduates from Harvard with bachelor's degree.

1917	Begins work toward master's degree at Columbia; studies under Brander Matthews.
1918	Awarded master's degree. Rejects offer of teaching appointment at the University of Minnesota. Spends next two years with *The New York Times*.
1920	Engages briefly in publicity work for a Texas oil man; begins an association with playwright Kenyon Nicholson.
1925	Reaches low point in "material condition and in morale." Unable to make a living.
1927	*The Second Man* produced with the Lunts in the leading roles.
1929	*Serena Blandish* and *Meteor* both open in New York. Friend and mentor Daniel Asher commits suicide that winter.
1930	Writing for motion pictures in Hollywood.
1931	*Brief Moment* opens.
1932	*Biography* opens. Behrman continues heavy writing schedule in Hollywood.
1934	*Rain from Heaven* opens.
1936	*End of Summer* opens. Marries Elza Heifetz in Port Chester, New York.
1937	The Behrmans' only child, David Arthur, born in Salzburg, Austria.
1938	Behrman joins Playwrights' Company with Robert Sherwood, Maxwell Anderson, Elmer Rice, and Sidney Howard.
1939	*No Time for Comedy* opens.
1941	*The Talley Method* opens. Behrman works at the Metro-Goldwyn-Mayer studio in Culver City, California, with Greta Garbo.
1942	*The Pirate* opens. Behrman leaves California; locates in Ridgefield, Connecticut.
1943	Admitted to Department of Arts and Literature of the National Institute of Arts and Letters.
1944	*Jacobowsky and the Colonel* opens and wins the New York Drama Critics Award as the best foreign play of the season. Behrman goes to England on assignment from *The New Yorker*.
1945	*Dunnigan's Daughter* opens. Behrman withdraws himself and his play from The Playwrights' Company.
1949	*I Know My Love* opens. Behrman receives honorary degree from Clark University.

1952 *Jane* opens. *Duveen* published.
1954 *Fanny* opens. *The Worcester Account* published.
1958 *The Cold Wind and the Warm* opens.
1960 *Portrait of Max* published.
1962 *Lord Pengo* opens. Behrman receives Brandeis University Creative Arts Award. Appointed trustee of Clark University.
1964 *But for Whom Charlie* opens; his final play.
1965 *The Suspended Drawing Room* published.
1968 *The Burning Glass* published.
1972 Behrman's memoirs, *People in a Diary*, published.
1973 Behrman dies of apparent heart failure on September 9 in New York.

CHAPTER 1

From Providence Street to Park Avenue

THE life and career of Samuel Nathaniel Behrman combine to form a particularly American story of success. His parents, Joseph and Zelda (Feingold) Behrman, had emigrated from Vilna in Russian Lithuania by way of Hamburg to New York sometime between 1890 and 1893; and they brought with them Hiram and Morris, their only two children at that time. As an orthodox Jew who had, in the words of S. N. Behrman, "lived under the shadow of a blood feud reaching back into the dim corridors of time,"[1] Joseph Behrman was keenly aware of the tradition of Jewish persecution, and he feared that in America he would not be able to observe faithfully the dietary laws of his religion.

I Worcester

Because some of Joseph's relatives had settled before him in the industrial city of Worcester, Massachusetts, he also took his family there. Upon his arrival, he arranged to occupy the dwelling on Water Street where S. N. Behrman was born. No official record of his third son's birth seems ever to have existed, and S. N. Behrman years later arbitrarily selected his own birthday: June 9, 1893. "I have long since forgotten the Hebrew date of my birth," he wrote many years later, "and my father's many-volume Talmud [into which his birthdate had been entered] was long ago given away. . . . I have made several attempts to get the official date of my birth from the City of Worcester, but without success; there is no record there of my ever having been born. But common sense tells me that 1893 must be reasonably close."[2]

Shortly after Behrman was born, a sister arrived who, as a small child, ran in front of a streetcar on Water Street and was fatally injured. Because she was never again spoken of in the Behrman household, her name has faded from memory. Mindful of the cause of her death, Joseph Behrman before long removed his wife and

three sons to nearby 31 Providence Street, where they inhabited a
tenement house which directly faced one synagogue and was close
to another. The Behrmans occupied the top floor of a typical Worcester "three decker" which still stands. The first two floors were
populated by the Cohens and the Feingolds, all relatives of the
Behrmans. For the time being, Joseph Behrman supported his family on the modest profits earned from his Water Street grocery
store.

The three Behrman sons found themselves caught in a conflict of
cultures. Their mother had almost no understanding of English, and
in the immediate neighborhood it was unusual to hear any language
except Yiddish. Unlike Behrman's uncles, who were all peddlers,
his father was recognized among the denizens of Worcester's Jewish
district as an ardent Talmudic scholar who devoted a portion of his
time to instructing children in Hebrew. S. N. Behrman later remembered him as "an unworldly, scholarly, casuistical, and nor-
mally gentle man with a supernatural imagination that dwelt mainly
on the hereafter."[3] Looking backward some sixty years later,
Behrman recalled his childhood in Worcester:

> There we were—my parents, my two older brothers, and I—a family
> uprooted from a veiled and ancient and unhappy past, and plumped down,
> unaccountably, in the tenement district of an industrial city in New En-
> gland. The American myths I acquired in my school history books—George
> Washington and the cherry tree, and the others—were thin and anemic
> compared to the Biblical exploits I had heard about at home. My father
> related the Old Testament stories as if they had taken place recently—as if
> they constituted his personal past.[4]

Behrman's first academic introduction to English came when he
was enrolled at the Providence Street School at the base of Providence Street hill. But, in 1903, at about the age of ten, he was
introduced to quite another aspect of his education when he and his
childhood friends happened to look into Mechanics' Hall where
Eugene V. Debs, the Socialist Labor party candidate for the presi-
dency of the United States, was delivering a speech. "We . . .
moved forward circumspectly, a row or two at a time until, when
Debs rose to speak, we were down under the platform and literally
at the speaker's feet," Behrman recalled. "Though I cannot remember a single word that Debs said that morning to his apathetic
audience and I never saw or heard him again, I am sure that this

chance visit gave to all my later life an orientation it would otherwise not have had—a bias in favor of those who had suffered from cruelty or callousness."[5] The impressions left by Debs on the young Behrman undoubtedly influenced the writer's general attitudes later on, especially his broad commitment to humanism and the varying degrees of distrust in capitalism that are to be found in such plays as *Meteor* (1929), *Biography* (1932), and *Wine of Choice* (1938).

Soon after the Debs experience, Behrman was introduced to the theater by his intimate schoolmate Daniel Asher, who appears as the character Willie Lavin in the autobiographical prose volume *The Worcester Account* and in the play based upon it, *The Cold Wind and the Warm*. Behrman and Asher witnessed a melodrama called *Devil's Island* at Lothrops's Opera House in 1904. Years afterward Behrman remembered that "it couldn't have been a very subtle play, and yet I hadn't understood it at all. This did not keep me from being thrilled by it. There was a miraculous scene at the end of the second act where the captain escaped from Devil's Island; you actually *saw* him getting into a boat and being rowed to a sloop waiting to transport him back to Paris. You even saw the sloop."[6]

When still in his fifteenth year, Behrman departed for New York without his parents' knowledge to spend four days with another schoolmate at the Mills Hotel on Thirty-sixth Street. The spectacle of the city, and especially that of the theater district, no doubt left an impression as strong as those he had acquired from Debs and the *Devil's Island* melodrama. As a consequence, Behrman was destined to spend most of his professional life in New York close to the literary and theatrical life that he loved.

Because of precarious health, two years elapsed between his departure from grammar school and his subsequent enrollment in Worcester's old Classical High School on Walnut Street. At about this time, he began to study piano after school with Asher's encouragement. Because of Behrman's general lack of physical coordination, his skill at the piano was little better than his prowess on the ball diamond. It was also at this time, however, that he began to explore not only his father's considerable Hebrew library but also the Worcester Free Public Library on Elm Street, two blocks from the high school. At the public library, Behrman's attention was attracted by a rather unlikely combination, Horatio Alger and Shakespeare. By the time he had reached high school, he could recite passages from *Hamlet* and *Macbeth* from memory; but, despite his budding literary interests, his scholastic achievement at this time was ordinary.

By the age of fifteen, Behrman had deepened his friendship with Asher, an intelligent, but emotionally unstable individual to whom he turned with his conflicts that arose from the contrast between his home life and the outside world. "There was no intellectual problem, no practical dilemma, no psychological crisis at home," Behrman once commented, "that I did not dump in [Asher's] lap. He became, so to say, my liaison officer between the medievalism of our household and the latter-day world; he understood both worlds and he enjoyed trying to reconcile them for me."[7] It was with Asher's encouragement, in fact, that Behrman first began to write. He later credited Asher with having gone "over all my manuscripts, analyzing them, correcting them, and taking endless trouble to prepare them for submission to, and, of course, eventual rejection by, various publications."[8] Asher, who became a businessman in Worcester, eventually took his own life in a Massachusetts mental hospital in 1929 when Behrman's professional career was scarcely underway.

Behrman heard a lecture by Sigmund Freud at Clark College in 1909, and remembered him years later simply as "a benignant old man." As a student at Clark years later, Behrman studied psychology under G. Stanley Hall, the man directly responsible for bringing Freud to Worcester. In that same year of Freud's visit, Behrman rode to Boston on a streetcar to view a production of George Bernard Shaw's *Caesar and Cleopatra* at the Park Street Theater. His response to the play was both enthusiastic and prophetic: "It had seduced me to the theatre. I thought it would be agreeable to write plays like that."[9] By the time Behrman was graduated from Classical High School, he clearly showed a talent for handling language, and his high-school introduction to Latin and Greek did no harm to his feeling for words.[10] Neither did his interest in oratory. Behrman's high-school record indicates that he was elected president of the Sumner Club, a debating organization in which he had once taken the affirmative position on whether or not capital punishment should be abolished.

II *Clark College*

Behrman toured on the Poli vaudeville circuit in 1911 for some months with two others in a skit he had written himself called "Playing a Part." The circuit included stops at numerous theatrical ports of call in Canada, New England, and finally at a New York vaudeville house on Fourteenth Street. His youthful odyssey ended, unfortunately, with the failure of his physical health, and he was obliged to return to a less glamorous way of life in Worcester, where, at the urging of his family and Asher, he enrolled at Clark College as a special student. Scarcely had he begun to attend classes, however, when his father died, at 31 Providence Street in October, 1912. Hiram and Morris Behrman, meanwhile, were in the process of forming their accounting firm in New York, and they were eventually called upon to sustain their playwright brother during some of the most trying stages of his early career.

While at Clark College, Behrman's inclinations toward reading and writing continued unabated. He soon had two brief personal essays published in *The Clark College Monthly*, where the better student compositions found their way into print. At the conclusion of his first year at Clark, he was chosen to compete in a commencement-week oratorical contest, although the outcome of the competition somehow went unrecorded. After his return to campus in 1913, he saw four more of his essays published, and he became one of seven assistants on Clark's publication board. That September he was elected vice president of the Menorah Society, which had the objectives of covering "in detail the history of Jewish people" and of providing "a forum where the culture and ideals of Hebrew literature" could be discussed.[11] His academic year was cut short, however, when he was suspended because of his refusal to attend physical education classes. Behrman reacted to the dismissal by applying for admission to summer school at Harvard.

After a rewarding summer in Cambridge, he decided to return to Clark, and there he drew attention to himself in three ways: as an actor, as a public speaker, and as a writer. He found his courses generally easy, and he learned that he could maintain academic respectability with a day or two of cramming. On Fraternity Night in May, 1915, Behrman represented the Menorah Society by giving a talk on modern Hebrew literature. A campus reporter noted that "the skillful handling of his subject, as well as the unusual elegance of [his] expression, brought Mr. Behrman enthusiastic applause from the appreciative crowd.[12] Deepening his involvement at Clark, Behrman joined the Socialist Club and continued to submit short essays to *The Clark College Monthly*. In one of these, "Psychology and the New Philosophy of the Theatre," he wrote of having examined some forty representative modern plays, some of them written by Henrik Ibsen, G. B. Shaw, Arthur Wing Pinero, August Strindberg, Maurice Maeterlinck, and the eighteenth-century playwright Gotthold Ephraim Lessing.

As a result of Behrman's interest in literature and the theater, he declared English as his major subject at Clark. Loring Holmes Dodd, a professor of English, later remembered Behrman as an able, vivacious, eager undergraduate: "He was the sort of student whose keen questioning in class was provocative of lively discussion. In my office for conference he was always diverting. The themes he passed in were almost entirely dialogue surprising for an undergraduate in its maturity, wit [and] sophistication . . . disappointment was keen when he did not return to Clark for his junior year."[13] Behrman's failure to return, however, was due to his continued refusal to report for physical education classes. Evidently anticipating his suspension, he composed a letter to his academic dean in which he announced his intention of returning to Harvard, where he hoped to enroll in Professor George Pierce Baker's English 47 playwriting course.

III   *Harvard and After*

In 1915, Behrman had his first smattering of commercial success when he sold a short story called "La Vie Parisienne" for fifteen dollars to *The Smart Set*, which was edited by George Jean Nathan and H. L. Mencken. Of greater significance, however, was his move into Weld Hall at Harvard for his junior year, which was financed in part by the Price Greenleaf aid and by the Elnathan Pratt Scholarship fund. Although the main object of his coming to Harvard was Baker's English 47 drama workshop, Behrman first enrolled in English 12, a composition course taught by Charles Townsend Copeland, then Boylston Professor of Rhetoric. Behrman found that the experience of reading his compositions to the gentle but formidable "Copey" in his Hollis Hall study was a considerable strain. Still, he profited from Copeland's experience and from his insistence that his students read daily the King James Bible for the beauty of its style.

Behrman had been admitted to English 12 with Copeland's prior permission, and it was with relief and excitement that shortly before his senior year he secured Professor Baker's permission to enter

English 47. It was also no small satisfaction to learn later that he was the only undergraduate admitted to the course. His spirit was soon dampened, however, when he and his friend Sidney Howard submitted plays to the Castle Square Prize competition offered by a Boston theater and neither was a successful contestant.

English 47 included an introduction by Professor Baker to the comedic theories of George Meredith. Although the course also involved the writing and production of plays, Behrman apparently remained mostly in the background and evidently did not continue to act in plays as he had at Clark, for his theatrical interest was now exclusively limited to the role of playwright. Years later, he looked back with wonder at the forces that prompted him to continue writing: "I began writing plays. I don't know why. Chiefly, I think, because I had no faint notion of the impossibility of marketing them! Had I any idea of the difficulties ahead, I must surely have stopped. But I didn't know and I kept on blindly. I wrote play after play: serious, farce, melodrama, comedy. They met a universal fate. But I kept on."[14]

After taking his bachelor's degree from Harvard, Behrman searched for work in newspaper offices in different cities, but with no success. "I found it impossible to get a job anywhere," Behrman later recalled. "I did some writing, selling an occasional article or short story to some parsimonious editor, but I hadn't any 'line,' and as I wanted some definite answer to people who asked me what I was doing, I enrolled for an A.M. degree at Columbia."[15] He lived with his brothers Hiram and Morris in Manhattan, where they had established their accounting office. While he was pleased in 1917 to have sold two short stories and an essay to *The Seven Arts*, *The New Republic*, and *The Touchstone*, the knowledge that part of his support came from his brothers Hiram (ten years older) and Morris (seven years older) was not conducive to the development of his self-confidence.

Behrman's fortunes did not improve, but neither did they worsen; for, while he sold more fiction to *The Liberator* and *The Smart Set*, he also took his master's degree from Columbia in 1918, after having submitted a thesis ridden with typographical errors and entitled "Lord Morley as a Literary Critic." Columbia had given him, Behrman once said, "an A.M. degree and some entertaining contacts with John Erskine and Brander Matthews, but little else."[16] The University of Minnesota offered him a salary of twelve hundred dollars to become an instructor, but Daniel Asher once again played the role of advisor and influenced Behrman to remain in New York and to continue writing. Instead of accepting the teaching appointment, Behrman spent the next two years with *The New York Times*, first as a typist of classified ads and later as a book reviewer.

The period before the sale of his first important play, *The Second Man* (1927), was a time of waiting for his artistic inclinations to ripen and be recognized. In 1919, he managed to market six stories, including "That Second Man" which appeared in the November issue of *The Smart Set* and which he later transformed into *The Second Man* after three weeks of labor in a borrowed room.

Behrman ended his association with *The New York Times* in 1920, but he continued to publish fiction while temporarily doing publicity work for an eccentric Texas oil man as well as for the publishers Ben Huebsch and Thomas Seltzer. By 1921, he had formed a valuable association with J. Kenyon Nicholson, an Indiana-born prose writer and playwright whose only noteworthy play, *The Barker*, made its Broadway debut in 1927, the same year that *The Second Man* opened. Eventually, the two men shared accommodations at a West Thirty-sixth Street rooming house where in 1922 they began to collaborate on plays and short fiction. The two worked on a play called "The American Way," which was never produced, although it remained under option by producer Jed Harris. They also wrote a one-act comedy, "Bedside Manners," but it too was never produced. In 1924, Hugh Ford attempted to produce off Broadway, a Behrman melodrama entitled "The Scant Pint," but the results were disappointing. "The Incompatibles," still another play, went unproduced. By the spring of 1925, as Behrman later wrote, "I reached a low point in my material condition and in morale. I had to face the fact that I was unable to make a living. I had to face even a more devastating fact: that I didn't have an idea to work on, for a writer a more appalling kind of poverty still. I remember walking on Fourteenth Street on a raw March day, facing a blank. I was really among the unemployed!"[17]

IV *The Turning Point*

The crucial turning point in Behrman's career came in 1926 when he was able to collaborate with the older, more experienced, and more established playwright Owen Davis on a play they called *The Man Who Forgot* which opened in Philadelphia. More significantly, however, Behrman was able to arrange a pre-Broadway tryout of *The Second Man* with the Lakewood Stock Company in Skowhegan, Maine. Later that same year *A Night's Work*, another Behrman-Nicholson effort, was produced in New York; and at this time producer Jed Harris offered Behrman the publicity assignment in New York for John V. A. Weaver's popular comedy *Love 'Em and Leave 'Em*, which he eagerly accepted. Finally in December, 1926, Behrman sailed to England in the company of Harris and another producer, Crosby Gaige, to publicize the London production of George Abbott and Philip Dunning's *Broadway*.

Behrman's greatest single career breakthrough occurred, however, when the Theatre Guild presented *The Second Man*, which Behrman dedicated to his brothers. Critical reaction to the play was favorable, and Behrman had the satisfaction of knowing that the rather arduous period of his apprenticeship had at last ended. Although he lived to see nineteen more of his plays acted on Broadway, he brooded for the time being over whether he would be able to maintain the theatrical touch that he had captured in *The Second Man*. Maurice Zolotow of *The New York Times* remembered Behrman at this point in his career as "a slim, dark-eyed, curly haired, intellectual chap, with a high forehead, rimless spectacles, and a brooding melancholy of a young Jewish intellectual,"[18] an appearance curiously unlike what might be expected of a comic playwright.

After 1927, Behrman could not resist the economic lure of writing motion-picture scripts in Hollywood; and it was also at this time that he formed a valuable association with Harold Ross of *The New Yorker*. It was Ross, and not the movie tycoons, who gave Behrman the continued opportunity to flourish as a serious writer. In 1929, for example, Ross commissioned Behrman to write a "profile" of George Gershwin, which was subsequently printed in *The New Yorker*, and this essay was the first of many that appeared there in the years to come.

In the summer of 1928, Behrman sailed again to England; and his purpose this time was to oversee the London opening of *The Second Man* with Noel Coward in the leading role. As time permitted, he worked on a play titled *A Love Story*, which was never produced. Two more plays, however, were being polished for the 1929 season: *Serena Blandish* and *Meteor*. But upon his return from London, Behrman was greeted with the news of Daniel Asher's suicide.

"Along with my grief," he wrote in 1954, "I felt a kind of terrible self-reproach; I could not repress the feeling that if I had been there I might, by some miracle of friendship, have held off the steep, dark walls that converged on [Asher] to extinguish him."[19]

Behrman spent most of the 1930s in Hollywood, where in 1930 alone he contributed to four screenplays including *Liliom* (based upon the play by Ferenc Molnar); *The Sea Wolf* (based upon the Jack London novel); *Lightnin*; and *He Knew Women*, a film version of *The Second Man*. From the outset, Behrman had misgivings about Hollywood and the kind of artistic reputation it was fostering. In his play *Biography* (1932), the radical Richard Kurt predicts that "in the new state men . . . won't have to prostitute themselves in Hollywood." Later in the same play the more philosophically mature Marion Froude refers to Hollywood as "the new Eldorado—art on the gold-rush." In spite of Behrman's true feelings about the motion-picture industry, he continued to labor diligently over more filmscripts; in 1931, he assisted with three more screenplays: *Surrender, Daddy Long Legs,* and *The Brat.* And, although *The New York Times* referred to Behrman cynically as "the Molnar of Malibu Beach,"[20] Behrman's heart was undoubtedly still with the New York stage where his *Brief Moment* opened in November, 1931.

By 1932 Behrman was at work on three fronts: there were still more motion-picture contracts (*Rebecca of Sunnybrook Farm* and *Tess of the Storm Country*); three more essays were published in *The New Yorker*; and his latest Broadway play, *Biography*, opened. There were still four more films in 1933: *Cavalcade, Hallelujah I'm a Bum, My Lips Betray*, and the adaptation of his play *Brief Moment.* While 1934 proved to be a profitable year because of the New York reception of *Rain From Heaven,* Behrman's time was largely devoted to three more pictures. One of these, *Biography of a Bachelor Girl*, was an Anita Loos adaptation of his own *Biography.* Another was *Queen Christina*, with Greta Garbo in the leading role. A third, *As Husbands Go*, was based on a drama by Rachel Crothers.

Behrman was now inclined to be somewhat defensive about Hollywood. In a 1934 interview with *The New York Times*, he said that "picture writing [was] one of the hardest jobs in the world."[21] Later that month in *The New Yorker*, he published a reply to such anti-Hollywood critics as Edmund Wilson, Sidney Howard, and George Bernard Shaw. Conceding "that pictures [were] a mob art," Behrman argued that, "without exception, the Hollywood satirists

—except when they are, as they reproach the producers for being, frankly commercial—are either academic or unfair." As for the possibility of motion pictures as art, he concluded, "there [was] no reason [why] someone shouldn't come along who might use this extraordinary medium with a Shakespearian fullness."[22]

Feeling perhaps less self-conscious about his liaison with the filmmakers, Behrman continued to work sporadically in Hollywood. Between 1935 and Pearl Harbor, he had a hand in the script preparation of nine more pictures: *Anna Karenina* (1935), *A Tale of Two Cities* (1935), *Conquest* (1937), *Parnell* (1937), *The Cowboy and the Lady* (1938), *Ninotchka* (1939), *No Time for Comedy* (1940), *Waterloo Bridge* (1940), and *The Two-Faced Woman* (1941). Except for five widely separated Hollywood assignments after 1948, Behrman's uneasy alliance with the movies had finally come to an end.

His real interest and enthusiasm in the 1930s was writing for the stage; and, while he remained the prisoner of Hollywood, his plays appeared in New York with great regularity. *End of Summer* with the irresistible Ina Claire had opened in February, 1936; and it was followed by *Amphitryon 38* with Alfred Lunt and Lynn Fontanne in 1937. *Wine of Choice*, with Alexander Woollcott, opened the year after. Katherine Cornell and Laurence Olivier played in *No Time for Comedy* in the spring of 1939; and the last of the prewar plays, *The Talley Method*, featured Ina Claire in February, 1941, at Henry Miller's Theatre.

Behind the scenes, Behrman's private life was changing as rapidly as his career. In a quiet but publicized ceremony at Port Chester, New York, he was married on June 22, 1936, to Elza Heifetz, sister of the violin virtuoso. Partly because of Elza's friendship with Arturo Toscanini, the Behrmans were in Salzburg for the music festival of 1937, although the occasion was rendered bleak by the burgeoning Nazi menace. It was in Salzburg, however, the the Behrman's first and only child, David Arthur, was born. The recollection of Hollywood, New York, and Salzburg later provided the setting for Behrman's long-contemplated novel, *The Burning Glass*, published in 1968.

After Behrman's return to America, he was approached by Sidney Howard about the formation of the Playwrights' Company, the object of which was to remove some of the financial risk of play production by sharing the burden with other writers whose work would be produced by the group over a period of time. In an interview with

The New York Times about the new association, Behrman's stress
was on the practical aspect of it: "It is better business to spread one's
risk over the continuing work of five men than to put one's whole
stake each time upon the single work of an individual."[23] His next
three productions—*No Time for Comedy, The Talley Method,* and
The Pirate (1942)—were all presented by the Playwrights' Company, although it meant a reluctant break between Behrman and the
Theatre Guild, which had produced his earlier work. His new affilia-
tion with the Playwrights' Company was destined to continue until
1945 when he withdrew himself and his new play, *Dunnigan's
Daughter,* from the group because he began to recognize that the
company had become a separate entity, as well as an encroachment
upon his own artistic expression.

At the outbreak of World War II, Behrman was on the Culver
City lot of Metro-Goldwyn-Mayer preparing Greta Garbo's script
for *The Two-Faced Woman,* a film later condemned as "immoral" by
the Legion of Decency. From his desk, he wrote of "the long dis-
equilibrium of our generation" that had been so apparent to him
during his Austrian trip. "When, as I hope, my little boy, born four
years ago in what was Austria, grows up to enter Harvard," he
continued optimistically, "the social order will be on a firmer, more
realistic basis than any we have known."[24]

For the moment, however, his spirits were darkened by the reports of Hitler's advancing armies and by persistent rumors of a
pending Japanese attack on the California coast. His commitment
with the moviemakers concluded for the time being, Behrman
longed to return to the East where in January, 1942, he negotiated
the purchase of an estate in Ridgefield, Connecticut, that consisted,
The New York Times reported, of "forty-six acres, with a frame
colonial residence containing five masterbedrooms, five servant's
rooms, a three car garage with living quarters, a large barn and
other outbuildings."[25] This estate was indeed a far cry from the
tenement dwelling of his youth, but his financial success had
equaled that of some of his characters portrayed in the plays of the
1930s.

Even with his own economic security insured, Behrman's developing social conscience caused him to brood about the prolifera-
tion of fascism and to aid the cause of freedom in any way possible.
When *No Time for Comedy* played in England in 1941, Behrman
donated his royalties to the British Red Cross. On still other occa-

sions he prepared radioscripts in support of the Allied war effort. In recognition of his artistic achievements, he was elected to the Department of Arts and Literature of the National Institute of Arts and Letters in 1943, an honor which bolstered the self-confidence he had lacked in the 1930s when he had feared privately that his successes were real only in an economic sense. The following year, 1944, the year of his mother's death, Behrman replaced Clifford Odets as the adapter of Franz Werfel's *Jacobowsky and the Colonel*, which won the New York Drama Critics' Award as the best foreign play of that season.

V The New Yorker

Between 1935 and 1944, Behrman's output of prose essays, which had been overshadowed by the demands of motion picture and stage writing, reached a bare minimum; for only three of his essays were published in *The New Yorker* in this period. His character Clark Storey in *The Second Man* had paid high tribute to "the good prose of the English masters," calling it "solid, clear, sometimes hovering close to poetry—but in the main sensible and intelligent and—well-behaved." After Harold Ross invited Behrman to record his impressions of wartime England for *The New Yorker* in 1944 and again in 1946, the pieces Behrman wrote certainly seemed to possess the virtues that Clark Storey had extolled.

When Behrman published "Mr. Lavin, Mr. Lupkin, and Dr. Abercrombie" in *The New Yorker* in the summer of 1946, the essay became the first of eleven parts that later were brought together in his autobiographical remembrance *The Worcester Account* (1954). In 1951 (the year of Harold Ross's death), he wrote a series of articles serialized in *The New Yorker* under the general title "The Days of Duveen," which were subsequently reissued in hardcover as *Duveen* that same year. His incisive treatment of Joseph Duveen's career as an international dealer in art treasures in some ways paralleled Behrman's own ascendancy as a man of letters. As he worked on "The Days of Duveen" series in 1950, an offer from Metro-Goldwyn-Mayer to collaborate on the script for *Quo Vadis* once again took Behrman to Hollywood.

Behrman's *Portrait of Max* also had its origin in *The New Yorker*, where it was published in serial form in the spring of 1960. By now it was clear that, while his interest in the theater had not altogether lapsed after the end of World War II, he was never again to write for

Broadway with quite the persistence that he had had between 1927
and 1945. Following the war, he worked intermittently on his play *I
Know My Love*, which he had written expressly for his friends the
Lunts, and the production finally opened in 1949. After 1945 he also
labored over repeated versions of the play *Jane*, which he had
adapted from the short story of the same name by Somerset
Maugham. *Jane* opened in February, 1952, in New York with Edna
Best and Basil Rathbone in the principal roles under the direction of
Cyril Ritchard.

The musical play *Fanny* (1954) catered more to public taste for
romantic, sentimental, light entertainment than any play that
Behrman had worked on before. With a huge cast headed by Flor-
ence Henderson and Walter Slezak and with music and lyrics provided by Harold Rome, *Fanny* became a box-office success; and the
film version issued in 1961 gave the play ample additional exposure.
After *Fanny*, however, Behrman tended to limit his activities. He
reviewed books for *The New Yorker*, to which in 1956 he also contributed a short story with the somewhat forbidding title of "The
History of the Russian Revolution." After seeing the story into print,
he returned to Hollywood once more to prepare the scripts for
Françoise Sagan's *A Certain Smile* and for a film based upon
Jacobowsky and the Colonel, which was retitled, for movie audiences, *Me and the Colonel*.

The Cold Wind and the Warm, an autobiographical play
suggested by *The Worcester Account*, opened in 1958, and, although the critics gave it only lukewarm reviews, it was undoubtedly Behrman's finest dramatic achievement in a very long career.
Two more plays were yet to come, but neither would reach a comparable dramatic power: Behrman transformed *Duveen* into a play
called *Lord Pengo*, which was produced in 1962 with Agnes
Moorhead, Charles Boyer, and Henry Daniell; and his final play,
But for Whom Charlie, evoked little response from theatrical critics
when it appeared at the Lincoln Center in 1964. When the play
closed, Behrman had reached the age of seventy-one. Owing no
doubt to the reception of the play and to his advancing age, he at last
ceased writing for the stage.

VI *Aftermath*

Besides having insured himself a place in the development of the
American theater, Behrman had been amply rewarded by recogni-

tion and by financial return. His honorary Doctor of Laws conferred at Clark University in 1949 was followed by his appointment as an alumni trustee from 1962 until 1968. In 1962, he was awarded the Brandeis University Creative Arts Award; and at this time he gave his lifetime collection of theater memorabilia—consisting of manuscripts, programs, notes, letters, telegrams, and reviews—to the Wisconsin Center for Theater Research. Following his seventieth birthday, Behrman suffered a stroke while on a brief holiday from his Park Avenue apartment; and he was partly debilitated from that time onward. Even then, however, he planned to write two ambitious autobiographical pieces: a novel, *The Burning Glass* (1968), which appeared in the author's seventy-fifth year; and a series of memoirs printed under the title *People in a Diary* in *The New Yorker* in May, 1972. "Perhaps a lifelong preoccupation with the arts can be a powerful factor in longevity," he speculated toward the end of his life.[26]

"Sam" Behrman, as he was known to his close friends, died of apparent heart failure on Sunday, September 9, 1973. Eloquent tributes to his memory appeared in newspapers and magazines around the country and overseas, but probably none was so effectively to the point as that in "The Talk of the Town" column in *The New Yorker* on September 24:

Some days ago, S. N. Behrman died, at the age of eighty. The space he occupied was more than that of one man, and with his death this crowded city seemed suddenly vacant. Decade after decade, his brilliant writings kept streaming down from wherever he lived uptown—plays, articles, fiction, memoirs—and, for those who were lucky enough to be his friends, his talk flowed along in parallel bounty and with equal brilliance. A telephone call from Sam Behrman was an event; he could be as inventive and witty on the telephone as he could be on paper. A lunch or tea or companionable evening with him was an even bigger event; he had an endless supply of stories to tell, and they tended to be funnier than anyone else's stories.

The tribute concluded with some remarks on Behrman's last days: "Immobilized, nearly sightless, he sat in his room and sent out messages to his friends—to the world, really. It was true that he still cared deeply about what was going wrong, he still thought most things were funny, and he wished us well."

CHAPTER 2

The Years of Apprenticeship

I N spite of virtually a lifelong devotion to literature and writing
S. N. Behrman developed very slowly as a writer, and his talent
was unquestionably late in blooming. A survey of Behrman's writing
of any kind before 1927 indicates that he was more determined than
accomplished and that both his ideas and his thoughts required a
comparatively extended period of time to become fully confident
and sophisticated. Although *The Second Man*, his first commercially
successful play, was produced in 1927, he still needed to wait until
the 1930s for the best of his plays to appear and until the 1940s for
the best of his prose to appear in the pages of *The New Yorker*.
While his abilities awaited the necessary seasoning and refinement,
they did not emerge without a good deal of sustained, concerted
effort in the face of continued discouragement.

Scarcely any of Behrman's writing prior to 1927 is readily accessi-
ble to the casual reader without a search into the musty back num-
bers of the popular magazines of the early 1900s. To add to the
difficulty, much of Behrman's writing, especially his early exercises
in playwriting, were unpublished; and those that were published
are exceedingly difficult to locate today. Nonetheless, any com-
prehension of S. N. Behrman's mature style and outlook must begin
with a glimpse at his earliest work. Moreover, it is necessary to bear
in mind that Behrman was from first to last a prose essayist, notwithstanding his tireless ambitions as a playwright. Before 1927, he
wrote far more prose than drama; and the same pattern persisted
throughout the final three decades of his life, when such accomplished books as *Duveen, The Worcester Account, Portrait of
Max, The Suspended Drawing Room*, and *People in a Diary* far
exceeded the general quantity and the quality of his plays. To
examine the full range of Behrman's writing is to reach the conclusion that he was an essayist enchanted with the theater.

I *Early Themes and Preoccupations*

It is less than surprising that certain themes and attitudes that Behrman embraced as a young man gradually disappeared but that others became a part of his mature outlook. The early writing repeatedly shows an obsession with the American passion for rising materially in the world. It is quite clear in almost all that Behrman ever wrote that something always remained of the poor but capable Jewish boy from Worcester who was struggling to break free from his social and economic limitations into a fuller, richer, more rewarding life. Behrman would always be, in the best sense of the word, ambitious; and his concern for getting ahead in the world is particularly evident in his earlier writing in which the characters are not infrequently questing after wealth. As time moves on, however, Behrman characters gradually quest more for self-understanding rather than for economic rewards. Consciously or not, the Alger stories that Behrman had read so voraciously during his youth appear to have left their imprint on his own vision of the American success myth.

Among the earliest compositions Behrman ever published was a three-paragraph essay in *The Clark College Monthly* for December, 1912. "Culture and Shaves" tells of a German barber in Worcester who had "worked for twenty years, without a vacation, [to afford] a three month's visit to his beloved *Vaterland*." The nineteen-year-old Behrman ends his anecdote by remarking about how commendable it is to reach one's goal by dint of sustained, personal effort, and he concludes, "Could any tribute be more eloquent!" Similarly, in another essay printed in the college monthly in January, 1913, Behrman spoke of having seen the performance of a youthful violin virtuoso. The performer, although "a mere boy," had won international fame and had come from Russia to America to perform. Behrman is impressed by the youth's innate genius, by his foreign background, and by his meteoric ascendancy as an accomplished performer. It was expressly this kind of realized ambition that appealed to Behrman not only as a young college student but as a man, as, for example, the portraits in *The Suspended Drawing Room* tend to illustrate.

One of Behrman's first short stories, "The Song of Ariel," printed in the May, 1917, issue of *The Seven Arts* leads to some of the same conclusions about being a success in life, but the approach to these conclusions is somewhat different. In this story, Behrman emphasizes what becomes of a person who does not, in fact, realize his dreams; the outcome is bitter frustration and disappointment. The protagonist in the story fails to receive the substantial pay raise he has been contemplating, and, as a result, his life falls totally into ruin. The tale is a slight one, but its point is clear. Similarly, "The Coming of the Lord: A War Story," printed in *The Touchstone* that October, depicts once again the psychologically destructive effects that result from the failure to attain one's ambitions. In this instance, a recently arrived immigrant in New York is, to his great disappointment, denied the opportunity of enlisting to serve in World War I because of a physical disability.

But "it wasn't how you began, it was how you finished that counted," the protagonist concludes in "Tawny Makes a Visit," published in *The Smart Set* (March, 1919); and this point of view prevails often in Behrman's early work. Eventually, Behrman modified this general view in *Meteor* (1929), in which he demonstrated that "success" can be as devastating as failure. For the time being, however, his thought had not come this far. In a story called "The Honorary Pall-Bearers Were—," which *The Smart Set* carried in April, 1919, he depicted a man who had done well in the newspaper business through the conventional pattern of "getting ahead" in America. The protagonist in this story has "married a girl who had enough money to by a small paper" which he, in time, "made . . . a big paper."

Almost anywhere in Behrman's apprenticeship writing, the subject of succeeding materially is foremost in his mind. "That Second Man" (*The Smart Set*, November, 1919) involves for example, one man's jealousy of another over "the place [the latter] had won for himself in the intellectual world" and over the wealth that has been acquired because of it. Occasionally Behrman's sense of competition for wealth and prestige tends to neutralize his emerging anticapitalistic opinions. For example, in August, 1919, he published an essay entitled "The Advertising Man" in *The New Republic* in which he celebrated the successful advertising man whose "salary is twice that of the President of the University from which he didn't graduate." The suggestion is, of course, that what the man lacks in intellectual sophistication, he makes up in dollars.

By the 1920s, Behrman had become suspicious of the headlong drive for wealth that he saw around him. In a story named "Hickey and Mother Goose," published in *The Liberator* in March, 1920, he wrote about the plight of a returned World War I soldier who for a time sells souvenir German military helmets on the streets of New York. He is pleased to see that at the outset of his venture "money began to shower in on him, like roses on a triumphal parade." Not long after, however, his enterprise fails, as does his belief in the capitalistic system. In August of that same year, Behrman had grown more sardonic about the meaning of success when he published a closet drama in *The Smart Set* called "Never Stretch your Legs in a Taxi," in which he sketched a scene between a poet and his companion where the two discuss success in the arts. Success, the companion avers, is a fragile commodity: "Your poetry had made a unique place for you," for "every breath you draw endangers your reputation."

The problem of success in a competitive world led Behrman to other, but related themes in his writing. Not infrequently, for example, a young man's hoped-for success in the world is closely bound to other factors. Matrimony is one, and it figures ambiguously in the apprenticeship pieces; for not infrequently the prospect of marriage becomes an all but insuperable barrier to a young man's achieving his goals in life. It therefore behooves the really ambitious man to shun women for fear that they will stand in his way by denying him the personal freedom he needs to achieve his ends. Under other circumstances, however, marriage becomes the great gateway to opportunity, as is the case with the young man who marries the girl with enough money "to buy a small paper." But, when marriage becomes one more step in the realization of one's private ambitions, obvious moral questions arise; and these are expressly treated in such plays as *Serena Blandish*, *End of Summer*, and *Jane*, in which persons who marry for money are ridiculed.

II   *Men, Beware Women*

As a young man, Behrman viewed women as emotional snares and as dangerous emotional and economic risks. In 1912, for example, his somewhat prudish essay "Park-Bench Lovers" in *The Clark College Monthly* deplored with some indignation the practice of couples retiring "to the public parks to give vent to their protestations of affection." A year later, the college monthly printed his bitter short story "The Man Who Hated" about a convict who, after his release from prison, finds that his wife has left him for another

man. Continuing to warn against the dangers of contact with women, Behrman wrote a review of Eugène Brieux's play *Damaged
Goods* for *The Clark College Monthly* in December, 1913, in which
he approved the play's sermon against the threat of venereal dis-
ease; he offered the hope that the play may "have succeeded in
keeping some of Boston's young men from the stage doors of the
burlesque theatres." His tendency to beware of women figured
again in "The Destroyer," a play written for *The Clark College
Monthly* in April, 1914. His play was an Ibsenesque account of an
outrageously flirtatious wife, and part of the point, once again, was
that women are not to be trusted. More than three years later in
"Movie Morals," an essay he contributed to *The New Republic* (August, 1917) Behrman noted with apparent approval that "it is one of
the canons of movie morality that no woman can have relations with
a man outside of wedlock without coming, sooner or later, as a direct
result of her delinquency, to some dire fate, preferably death."

Young David Hannes in "The Coming of the Lord" is one of
Behrman's early characters who avoids trouble by avoiding women.
"Girls frightened him," the narrator comments. The short story
"Surrender" (*The Liberator*, May, 1918) indicates the consequences
of casting one's lot with a woman, but the plot is somewhat shop-
worn: a young woman becomes pregnant; and, although her young
lover would prefer to evade his responsibility to her by enlisting in
the army, he forthrightly, if reluctantly, agrees to marry her before
he reports for induction. Yet here and elsewhere marriage is approached with a certain trepidation, as in "The Return," a story
published in *The Smart Set* (November, 1918) which shows a father
who returns after an absence of fifteen years to catch a glimpse of his
daughter and who remembers that marriage had been "intolerable"
for him and that, while married, "every task was a burden, life a
matter for complaint." In "Tawny Makes a Visit" the protagonist,
who attends the marriage ceremony of his sweetheart and his best
friend, hears the bishop proclaim that matrimony is "an honorable
estate"; and he asks himself, "did the Bishop really believe that?
Hadn't he read Shaw?"

There can be no question that Behrman caused his women
characters to fare badly in a number of the apprenticeship pieces. In
the story "The Wraith" (*The Smart Set*, November, 1920), he depicted a flawed love affair wherein his female character suffers the
most. In another story printed in *The Smart Set*, "Rupert Goes on

the Loose" (March, 1922), Behrman wrote of three vindictive spinsters who hound a young college instructor out of a small town. The instructor, meanwhile, is in the process of writing a novel "about a young man who doesn't get on very well with women." In the story "Holiday," written by Behrman and Nicholson, a young provincial working girl's brief excursion to an Indiana summer resort in search of romance ends in the bitterest kind of disillusionment. And in still another story written in collaboration with Nicholson, "Loan Exhibit," (*The Smart Set*, June, 1923) there is a clandestine romance between a married woman and an artist which ends in severe disappointment. One more suffering woman who appears in "The Bathroom Key," written by Behrman and Nicholson and published in *The Smart Set* for April, 1923, is driven to suicide by the general misery of her life. In a word, women seem to spell trouble of one sort or another in these early specimens of Behrman's writing. Their lives are linked with unfaithfulness, disappointment, disillusionment, and needless encumbrance. Except for the eventual development of the knowing, wise, emancipated woman in Behrman's later writing, his distrust of women and their ways is always present.

III *The Emergence of a Social Conscience*

The apprenticeship pieces reveal a gradually sharpened awareness in Behrman of pressing social and political questions, but not until the 1930s did Behrman feel obliged to comment about the serious moral issues of his day, especially those arising from the Depression and from the growth of fascism in Europe. Ultimately, he assumed a political stance that favored neither the Left nor the Right; but, as a younger man, he wrote with a clear preference for the Left. "The Song of Ariel" is an obvious example of early twentieth-century naturalistic proletarian fiction, and it centers around a young New York office worker who is "in the service" of the "heroic deities" of commerce and industry but who is oppressed by the whole economic system which he supports. Because of the war, he gets no pay increase; because of no pay increase, his matrimonial plans are dashed. Discouraged, he consorts with the journalist Fred Rudnor, a man who is "not unknown" among radical elements in the city.

Another proletarian tale, "The Coming of the Lord," shows a similar young man who labors in a posh New York tailoring shop sewing smoking jackets destined to be worn by "the rich lawyers

and the rich brokers, for the steel-magnates and the society idlers,
for the matinee idols and the panders, from California to Maine."
The young worker, full of patriotism and faith in the American
Dream, becomes the object of a political conversion on the part of
his co-workers, who do everything possible to teach him about the
"struggle of the workingman for emancipation [and] the vast conception of class solidarity transcending national boundaries."

Not surprisingly, because of Behrman's radical sympathy, there is
a good deal of anticonservative sentiment in the early pieces. The
scene of "The Honorary Pall-Bearers Were—" is the funeral of an
influential big-city newspaper editor, a "hard-headed conservative"
who is regarded by the radicals as "the hoarse voice of the vested
interests." On other occasions, Behrman attacked conservatives in
his book reviews. In "Rupert Hughes and Karl Marx" (*The New
Republic*, July, 1919) a review of Rupert Hughes's *The Cup of Fury*,
Behrman objected to the novelist's prejudicial treatment of radicals.
The book's leading character, he wrote, "embodies all the popular
superstitions about the radical as atheistic, lazy, polygamous—and
unwashed." He then asks "whether Mr. Hughes [had] read any of
Marx's other writings." Only a month later, in Behrman's review of
Chase Osborn's *The Iron Hunter* ("Iron," *The New Republic*, August, 1919) Behrman pointed with disapproval to Osborn's description of Detroit politics, one in which "social reformers were anarchists," and "a disciple of Karl Marx and Rudolph [?] Engels was
crazy."

Behrman turned to heavy-handed satire of right-wing causes in
"Hickey and Mother Goose" in which a returned soldier from World
War I finds plenty of rightist causes to fight for on the home front:

There was still loyal work to be done for the flag right in New York City.
There was, for example, an insidious attempt on the part of the Kaiser to
revive an opera in his own dialect. Hickey and his friends were on hand to
see that this attack on the flag was nipped in the bud. And there were
meetings of the Anarchists, Socialists and Bolshevists to be suppressed.
They were all alike to Hickey: the finer distinctions in economics and
philosophy did not interest him. All he cared for was the fact that these
groups were as dangerous to the country as the Huns. . . .

The same intensity of satire prevails in "Never Stretch Your Legs
in a Taxi" in which two men argue (somewhat facetiously) the Marxist line over who should pay for the repair of a broken cab window.

One character explains to his disgruntled taxi driver that his friend "is a Communist. He does not recognise the existence of private property." In time, the friend speaks for himself: "Ultimate ownership is like ultimate responsibility, impossible to trace to its sources." Behrman, however, never overtly advocated Marxian economics; but in his mature years he repeatedly argued for tolerance toward ostensibly "subversive" ideas. Despite pleas for toleration, his satirical thrusts at the right seldom ceased; for the principle of tolerance became more important to him than the object of it. He remained convinced that the closed mind poses a greater threat to civilized life than any subversive philosophical ideas possibly could.

IV *Into the Future*

Two of Behrman's earliest thematic preoccupations, his concern with success and his wary attitude toward women, survived in a modified form in his later writing. Plays such as *The Second Man*, *Meteor*, and *Serena Blandish*, to cite only three, are still very much concerned with the prospects of succeeding in life and with the problems that marriage can bring. Still other ideas that would later emerge as major themes are, for the time being, scarcely stressed at all; for example, Behrman's concern for the welfare of Jews and his celebration of Jewish life had to wait until the 1930s and 1940s. Jewish workmen are referred to in his story "The Coming of the Lord" (1917), but elsewhere there is scarcely any concern expressed about Jewish characters and culture. Not until the full-scale revival of anti-Semitism brought about by Hitler's Germany did Behrman's overt concern for Jews appear in his writings.

The theme of friendship, so significant in his later work, also required time to develop. In the early pieces, his characters function in isolation, as is apparent in such stories as "The Man Who Hated" (1913) and "The Song of Ariel" (1917). In "The Coming of the Lord" (1917), the main character stands alone, isolated from his fellow workers. "The Return" (1918) has as its protagonist a man who is decidedly cut apart from society, and "Tawny Makes a Visit" (1919) depicts a forsaken character who ventures out of a sickbed alone into the city streets. The concluding scene of his story "That Second Man" (1919) involves a marriage ceremony that alienates the main character and condemns him, apparently, to a life filled with solitude and loneliness.

"The Wraith" (1920) involves another detached protagonist, as does

"Rupert Goes on the Loose" (1922) and "Holiday" (1922). Ellen
Timme, one of the characters in "The Bathroom Key" (*The Smart
Set*, April, 1923), finds her solitary life so unbearable that she as-
phyxiates herself in a dreary rooming house. Eventually, however,
Behrman characters place a great deal of value on friendship and
loyalty. The role of the confidant becomes apparent in the better
plays beginning with *The Second Man*. The central characters in
*Serena Blandish, Brief Moment, Biography, End of Summer, Dun-
nigan's Daughter, Jane,* and *The Cold Wind and the Warm* find
themselves in the company of friends and friendly advisors.

One of Behrman's growing preoccupations after 1926 was the
conflict between generations; but, as a younger writer, he seemed
to have little concern for the friction between young and old, except
in two of his short stories. The first of these, "The Return," published when Behrman was twenty-five, contains a scene in which a
father looks disapprovingly at his teenage daughter. He finds her
"dressed in the exaggerated, copied mode affected by shopgirls on
their holidays. . . . Such clothes [impress him as having] an almost
painful incongruity. . . . She was not the reticent, shy child he had
pictured. She had a disquieting urban assurance, a too-easy sophistication." In the second of the stories, "Loan Exhibit" (*The Smart
Set*, June 1923), a commercial illustrator named Ben Fulda has as his
specialty the drawing of "merciless cartoons" aimed at "the youth of
America." Such plays as *Meteor, Rain from Heaven, The Talley
Method,* and others, which were written much later in his career,
deal in greater depth with the problems arising from the differences
between youth and maturity.

V *The Somber Comedian*

There was little indication prior to 1927 that Behrman would one
day become famous as a writer of high, sophisticated comedy, because he showed but little comic inclination. "Never Stretch Your
Legs in a Taxi" and his one-act play *A Night's Work* (1926) contain a
few witty lines, but elsewhere there is little to evoke mirth or laughter. In *The Second Man*, Behrman discovered in himself a vein of
comedic ore that he was eventually able to mine in plays like *Amphitryon 38* and *Jane*. The generally humorless sobriety that had
characterized his early writing was never entirely to disappear, although Behrman's ability to combine serious themes with comic
techniques became one of his more attractive features, at least in the

eyes of a great many theatergoers. His awakened sense of humor brought with it a more liberal, more tolerant point of view which contrasts with that of early pieces such as "Rupert Goes on the Loose" (1922), which is notably intolerant and satiric in the manner of Sinclair Lewis; for example, the story pointedly mentions *Main Street* as evidence supporting the view that "you couldn't expect much of these small towns." In his later work (particularly *Biography*), intolerance itself is the object of repeated attack; but the attacks are delivered with an element of comic good-naturedness.

VI *The Emergence of a Style*

The polished and urbane style of Behrman's prose that is familiar to those who have read him in *The New Yorker* was, as has been mentioned, the product of unremitting work begun at around the age of fifteen under the supervision of Daniel Asher. In addition to his exposure to Professor Dodd of Clark College and to Professor Copeland of Harvard, the prevailing prose style of *The New Yorker* unavoidably influenced his writing of English prose. Coming as Behrman did from a home where only a limited amount of English was spoken, his devotion to reading, which was an interest that he maintained throughout his life, undoubtedly aided his development of his own distinctive style. But long before his finished style emerged, Behrman was writing in a markedly different manner. In his 1913 review of the play *Damaged Goods* for *The Clark College Monthly*, he seemed to strain at appearing a authoritative:

"Damaged Goods," it has been remarked, is a bad play. As a matter of fact, it is not a play at all—it is a sermon, singularly powerful, a thesis in dialogue, a tract—what you will—but it is not a play and has no place in the legitimate theatre. It might more fitly be read from the pulpit or in the clinic, save that in neither of these places, could so wide a public be reached—certainly not in the clinic, and in a church, so perfect a rendering as Mr. Bennett and his associates gave could not perhaps be afforded.

If the syntax of this passage had been stressed to its limits, the worst was yet to come. In another review for *The Clark College Monthly* (February, 1914), Behrman discussed Shaw's *Caesar and Cleopatra:*

A Caesar at fifty-four, hiding beneath the laurel of victory an incipient bald spot; a Caesar abstemious and dyspeptic, disdaining cushions stuffed with rose leaves, denying Lesbian wine and ordering "barley-water;" a Caesar masterful and kindly, quizzical and gracious, disenchanted and good-humored, a Caesar mellowed by time, and trial, and conquest, into a world-philosopher-poet, a Caesar of swelling prose apostrophes that have the singing qualities of a page from Shakespeare, the Caesar of Mommsen be it understood; a Cleopatra of sixteen calling Caesar "old gentleman;" a vixenish, artful, amorous, spiteful, designing, thoroughly life-like, little creature belonging to any century; Brittanus, Caesar's secretary, a present day, middle class Britisher à la Shaw (how he must have chuckled while creating this anachronism!) lugubriously scrupulous of the proprieties, flouting Caesar for his vari-colored clothing, recommending the British custom of wearing plain blue, symbolic of respectability that won't come [off?] Apollodorus, a ready-mouthed Sicilian art dealer, bristling with epithets of Art for Art's sake, and all the others down to the last sentinel, a brightly animated, thoroughly life-like, keen-witted crew. . . .

From such astonishingly glib, over-abundant undergraduate exuberance as this, his mature style gradually formed. Behrman's immediate problem in his early prose was to harness and modulate a number of excessively amplified characteristics. The over-emphasized self-assurance that filled his writing at Clark College was symptomatic of his lack of self-confidence; and his desire to sound oracular succeeded only in revealing his uncertainty. Even with these temporary problems, the raw materials for a firm and intelligent prose style were always present; for as the Clark College essays indicate, Behrman possessed the insight necessary to recognize, illuminate, and enlarge upon what might otherwise have been the insignificant detail and the ostensibly irrelevant anecdote. Such undergraduate essays as "Park-Bench Lovers," "Culture and Shaves," and "Via Music" are, for example, ingenius elaborations upon commonplace observations. "Never Stretch Your Legs in a Taxi," slight though it is, was suggested by an incident involving Behrman and his poet friend Siegfried Sassoon. Sassoon had accidentally damaged a New York taxi when he broke a partition window while stretching his legs. Part of Behrman's great talent for the essay form was his immense skill at turning other such humdrum experiences into brilliantly incisive prose essays.

Indeed, Behrman's later prose reveals a special mastery of observing and interpreting detail. For example, in part three of *People in a Diary*, which was printed in the May 27, 1972 issue of *The New Yorker*, Behrman wrote of having witnessed Oscar Karlweis's magnificent performance during the Boston engagement of *Jacob-owsky and the Colonel:*

> In front of me sat two elderly gentlemen of a type more frequently encountered in London than in this country—tall, slim, with narrow faces, keen eyes, and beautifully brushed silver hair. The first act had gone well, and Karlweis had captivated the audience, as he had done in New Haven. I wanted, if possible, to get a comment on the play from these two gentlemen. In the intermission, I walked up the aisle just behind them.
> 'You know,' said one, 'I think that fellow Karlweis . . . is Jewish.'
> There was a long pause. The other man took time to assimilate this bizarre fact. Then he said, 'Well . . . I don't mind.'

VII *Literary Influences*

Behrman tended to reflect his erudition in his writing, for one of his habits was to allow ideas suggested to him by other writers to enter his own work—titles, authors, literary characters, and allusions all found their way into his own finished work. His particular preferences in literature—Shakespeare, Ibsen, Shaw, Maugham, for example—not infrequently find mention in his plays and essays. Abetted by at least some understanding of Hebrew, Latin, Greek, French, German, and Yiddish, as well as by a major in English, his exposure to letters as a young man was uncommonly generous; moreover, Behrman was fortunate in his inheritance of his father's consuming bookishness.

As is not terribly uncommon with other writers, particularly young ones, Behrman was inclined to write about himself; and the development of his literary career may, in fact, be read in terms of his self-awareness. As far back as his "Park-Bench Lovers" essay in 1912, for example, Behrman found a way to represent himself, through his use of point of view, as a person of uncommonly good taste and intelligence. His essay on "Culture and Shaves," written in 1915, was designed in part to emphasize his cultivation and refinement. Eventually, all of the contributions he made to *The New Yorker* were somehow biographical in nature; and a sequential reading of these reveals that his own role changes gradually from observer to protagonist. In his first three books of prose—*The Suspended Drawing Room, Duveen,* and *Portrait of Max*—Behrman is in the role of observer; in the last three prose books—*The Worcester Account, The Burning Glass,* and *People in a Diary*—he becomes the protagonist. Not only does he become the protagonist, but he does so with ever greater focus and specificity. *The Worcester Account* consists of local color scenes from his childhood, but the emphasis is on persons other than himself. In *The Burning Glass*, he is decidedly the protagonist, but he has an assumed name. Finally, in *People in a Diary*, he wrote of his private world.

Apprenticeships, no doubt, are never entirely ended; and, although 1927 was the year that Behrman's career was finally launched as a playwright, he was not always able to insure that his plays would succeed artistically and economically on the stage. Nevertheless, Behrman was reasonably clear by this time about the kind of writer he desired to become: sophisticated, witty, and civilized—a man of letters to whom the intelligent, sensitive, and urbane would listen.

CHAPTER 3

The Prime Years

THE vintage Behrman plays are those seven produced on Broadway between 1927 and 1936; *The Second Man, Serena Blandish, Meteor, Brief Moment, Biography, Rain from Heaven,* and *End of Summer.* Commencing with *Amphytryon 38* (1937), the inherent quality of his plays tended generally to decline; but his best play, *The Cold Wind and the Warm,* did not appear until 1958. In the nine years beginning with *The Second Man,* Behrman's theatrical sense was at its keenest; and the seven plays of these years can be read as variations upon a central core of interrelated ideas and attitudes that were to undergo surprisingly little significant change in the years to come. The seven plays can, of course, be considered as comedies, although on occasion the comedy prevails in the loosest sense of the word. While most of Behrman's lines do not evoke howls of laughter, neither can they be considered within the range of tragedy. These plays are, in fact, particularly reflective of their unhappy time. Consequently, they become more serious between 1927 and 1936, while they remain generally within the province of the comic vision of life. Behrman never wrote pure comedy, if such exists anywhere; his sense of the comic arises from his adroitness at managing irony and sophistication in plays like *Serena Blandish, Biography,* and *End of Summer.*

Each play, with the exception of *The Second Man,* develops very little, if at all, in its plot. Plays such as *Biography, Rain from Heaven,* and *End of Summer* are all but plotless in the conventional sense. In place of vital plots, each with a clear progression, Behrman constructs anecdotal "situations" which are generated when characters with diverse views and backgrounds match wits with each other. The settings are usually sedate and refined, for Behrman always had a fondness for expensively outfitted apartments and for plush country homes. Frequently, a sizable cast of characters revolves loosely around a singularly attractive, usually emancipated woman who functions in the play as a catalyst and as the synthesizer of the other diverse satellite characters.

Behrman had long been an admirer of the acting talents of Alfred Lunt, which he considered superior to those of Lynn Fontanne; and Lunt is certain to have exerted a considerable influence over the Behrman style of writing plays. Maurice Zolotow alleges that, in 1922, the young and not yet established playwright had watched Lunt perform in Alfred Savior's *Banco* some twenty times in order to study Lunt's handling of high comedy.[1] Zolotow quotes Miss Fontanne as saying that, "when Berri was a young man, he saw Alfred in *Banco* and he went balmy over the performance. Formed such an attachment for Alfred's technique, he couldn't see me."[2]

Behrman himself has written about this influence, that after *The Second Man* and *Amphitryon 38*, the Lunts:

appeared in one additional play of mine, "Meteor," and two foreign adaptations—"The Pirate," based on the play by the German playwright Ludwig Fulda, and "I Know My Love," adapted from Marcel Achard's Paris hit "Après de Ma Blonde." With the Lunts, it was not easy to distinguish a hit from a failure, because whatever they did attracted large audiences. Robert Sherwood wrote a piece of doggerel that went "If you want a play to run many a munt, get Lynn Fontanne and Alfred Lunt." On the road, of course, the Lunts could do no wrong; business would be good as long as they cared to tour.[3]

I   The Second Man

Inevitably, Behrman could not resist the urge to interest the Lunts, or at least Alfred Lunt, in *The Second Man*. Lawrence Langner recalled the circumstances of the play's sale and subsequent rehearsal:

In the year 1926, I was called on the phone by the ubiquitous Harold Freedman who informed me that our playreader Courtenay Lemon had returned a play which he thought I should read; he added, rather shrewdly, that had I read it, it would have been returned. I read the play. It was *The Second Man* by S. N. Behrman; I liked it enormously, and enthusiastically recommended it to my colleagues. Theresa Helburn and Philip Moeller seconded my enthusiasm for the play, and soon we were in rehearsal with

Alfred Lunt, Lynn Fontanne, Earle Larimore and Margalo Gillmore. The play was well received and S. N. Behrman was launched on his career.[4]

Behrman, too, regarded his career as launched when the play opened on April 11, 1927, at the Guild Theatre in New York. *The Second Man,* with its one hundred and seventy-eight performances, remained as one of Behrman's lengthier runs. While the play is in many respects flippant and affected, it would, in the context of Behrman's full canon of comedies, be remembered as one of his freshest and most irresistibly vivacious plays. It also had the advantage of being the simplest and most cleanly wrought drama of them all; for it is happily free from the contrived, sometimes pointless complications of plot and situation that marred many of Behrman's later plays, such as *I Know My Love* (1949).

The title, and presumably the suggestion for the play, came from a letter written by Lord Leighton to his sister; but Behrman could never recall where he had ever run across the letter which reads: ". . . For, together with; and as it were behind, so much pleasurable emotion, there is always that other strange second man in me, calm, critical, observant, unmoved, blasé, odious." Accordingly, *The Second Man* is designed around a series of character contrasts. Clark Storey (played by Alfred Lunt in a purple suit) is a slick, parasitic, second-rate writer of poetry and fiction. Storey's foil is Austin Lowe, a first-rate chemist who, ironically, cannot manage to mix a drink. Mrs. Kendall Frayne, an attractive, emancipated, worldly wise, wealthy widow, finds her antithesis in the young, impulsive flapper Monica Grey, who is referred to in the play as "a Tennysonian ingenue with a Freudian patter." Both women are interested in Storey, but he is far too slippery to consider matrimony unless it brings with it some substantial fringe benefits. In the end, Monica is sensibly and appropriately paired off with Lowe; and Storey, in typical Behrman fashion, evades marriage altogether. As the play ends, he is attempting to interest Mrs. Frayne in an excursion along the Riviera.

Although not the best way of examining the play, the temptation is to consider *The Second Man* in biographical terms. Clark Storey can well be identified with the young S. N. Behrman. The name "Clark" seems surely to be an allusion to his early days as a student at Clark College. "Storey," obviously suggests fiction. In the first act, Storey remarks to Kendall that he has "enormous respect for

money" which, he says, can only be felt by those whose past was
"poverty-stricken and whose present—is precarious." Storey, with
his eye on economic rewards and with his persistent insecurity,
resembles the Behrman of the early and middle 1920s. At the conclusion of the second act, Storey explains to Monica Grey why he
could not seriously entertain any thoughts of marrying a poor girl; to
do so, would send him back to the dreary, unpromising existence
from which he had only recently escaped. "I can see us now—in a
cheap flat—you looking blowsy—with little wrinkles under your
eyes—and I in cheap shirts and cracked shoes—brooding in a room
over the corpse of my genius." No possibility exists that Storey will
permit matrimony to undermine his private ambitions.

If there is a little of the young Behrman in the character of Clark
Storey, Behrman was decidedly unsparing in his self-assessment.
"I'm an adventurer—intellectually and morally—an *arriviste* with
one virtue—honesty," Storey pronounces in act I. After Monica has
seen some of Storey's prose writing, she calls him "a butcher with
artistic leanings." Storey, with honesty as his one virtue, claims in
the same act to have had "a shallow literary education." Even so, he
lives in a manner that would not have seemed unattractive to
Behrman in the 1920s; he inhabits "a duplex apartment of a
studio-building on the West Side," his quarters are decorated with
exotic furnishings, and he takes his meals at smart restaurants or
orders them from room service. He circulates among the supposedly sophisticated international literati, and he lounges in his
apartment wearing a yellow silk-lined gown "with wide sleeves and
[a] brilliant sash." There can be no question that Storey is a satire on
the nimble, quick-witted literary fop.

The slight problems that are introduced in the play center around
money and marriage. *The Second Man,* along with *Serena Blandish*
and *End of Summer,* is a play in which matrimonial fortune hunting
is practiced unabashedly and openly. Money problems trouble
Storey a great deal, and he seems unable to manage what little he
has. The play can, in fact, be read in materialistic terms; for, like a
host of Behrman characters after him, Storey cares far more about
money than anything else, even artistic integrity; and his desire for
wealth seems to have higher priority than the advancement of his
slight literary talents. During the three acts of the play, Storey
accepts a sizable handout from both Austin Lowe and Kendall
Frayne; and he also admits toward the conclusion of the first scene

of the second act that he has received "five thousand dollars for [having written] a white-washed biography of a millionaire sweat-shop owner." In the scene that follows, he refers to himself metaphorically as "a highly speculative stock." Money, he says, is his "favorite subject."

Despite the materialistic motivations of Storey, *The Second Man,* one of the more comic of the comedies, is freer from any kind of social message or statement than any of the other plays. With *The Second Man,* Behrman temporarily shelved his social conscience and surrendered himself to the writing of a superficial, light, high comedy. No more the writer of proletarian short stories, and not yet the good-natured crusader for tolerance, he wanted nothing too "important" to interfere with the airy texture of his first important play. His protagonist Clark Storey mentions that he "used to sit in a garret and believe in socialism," but he no longer does so because "it didn't take me long to find out how easy it is to starve on Idealism." Such is the whole texture of the play: light and cynical. Storey proclaims that "it's the fashion nowadays to be flippant" as his companions listen to him at the close of the first act.

Like Clark Storey himself, *The Second Man* has a certain prevailing evasiveness built into it. The play bobs and weaves, avoiding any real confrontation with the social issues of the day—such as the mad malaise of postwar life that F. Scott Fitzgerald wrote about—except in the most general of ways. With the exception of Monica Grey and Austin Lowe, the characters are unusually pretentious: "What this country needs is a dilettante class," Storey assures everyone in the first act. Some of that pretentiousness wears off by the second scene of the second act when the characters indulge themselves in champagne. "*In vino veritas!*" he exclaims. "Drink only intensifies your mood." With the aid of alcohol, several ugly realities are unearthed. Austin loathes Storey's maddening superficiality. Storey is jealous of Austin's mind and (especially) his money. At the close of act II, Behrman has Storey at the piano pounding the keys "cruelly, in an ecstasy of self-revealment" while Monica "huddles in the chair to escape the flagellation of sound."

II   Serena Blandish

Theatrical producer Crosby Gaige commended Enid Bagnold's anonymously written novel *Serena Blandish, or The Difficulty of Getting Married* (1924) to Behrman. The playwright, who gradually became enthralled with the book's heightened subtlety and refined wit, shared Gaige's opinion that it had strong possibilities for theatrical adaptation. *The Second Man* had, after all, been a highly successful rendering of some of Behrman's own short fiction; and Behrman somehow recognized in Enid Bagnold a kindred spirit. What impressed him, he later wrote, was the novel's "irresistible style and humorous invention" as well as its "tough awareness of the metallic facts of life."[5] Visiting London in 1928 to see Noel Coward perform in *The Second Man*, Behrman also arranged to meet the novelist to discuss his contemplated dramatic version of her book. When he wrote a brief epistolary dedication of his play "To the Author of 'Serena Blandish'—" in 1933, he confessed to having been seduced by the novel's "innocent and insidious" quality, and then commented on the adjustments necessary to convert prose fiction into drama.

In dealing with Behrman's adaptations, it is not always easy to distinguish his artistic contribution from someone else's. *Serena Blandish*, however, contains enough characteristic elements of style and content that the play might well have had its genesis in Behrman's own mind. The setting—plush and elegant—is populated by pretentious and aristocratic socialites whose lives are unaffected by the tribulations of the world that lies outside their door. The subtitle, *The Difficulty of Getting Married*, identifies a familiar Behrman preoccupation: the problems encountered in attempting to contract an economically "good" marriage. This time Behrman was able to put some new angles into an old theme.

Serena Blandish, which calls to mind the myths of both Cinderella and Pygmalion, concerns Serena Blandish, a lovely, young woman who, although socially and economically disadvantaged, is rescued temporarily from her unpromising environment by the "middle-aged, exquisitely dressed Jewish gentleman" Sigmund Traub. Traub reveals himself to her as the wealthy proprietor of a London jewelry store, and he lends Serena a diamond ring on the theory that she will become a "living show-window" for his wares. Soon, with the aid of the comic Countess Flor di Folio, who maintains a menagerie of animals and humans, Serena is placed in sumptuous circumstances where she is exposed to the economically most promising marriage prospects—those who can well afford to lavish still more diamonds upon her.

Such contrived circumstances lead directly into the related dilemmas of money and marriage. In the second scene of act II, when the countess asks Serena what she desires most in life, her answer is "happiness." But Serena's mother, who has commented earlier that she herself is a failure because she married one, revises her daughter's reply to the Countess's question:

MRS. BLANDISH: Serena means money—to buy happiness.
COUNTESS: Ah! Now! Money! That is to say—security. That is to say—if you are a woman—marriage.
MRS. BLANDISH: [Autobiographically]. Marriage doesn't always bring money.
COUNTESS: But it must be a rich marriage. I have heard that the middle classes often marry for love and are saturated with sentimentality. . . .

A few lines later, the Countess reminds Serena that, in the end, success counts most of all: "Though it is better to marry young, best to marry a rich man, next best to marry a distinguished man, it is better to marry a crossing-sweeper than not to marry at all. Success, my dear. . . ." Ultimately, Serena marries no one at all.

Although Clark Storey's mercenary designs on Mrs. Kendall Frayne might have seemed wryly amusing to Behrman, he found nothing funny about the butler Martin, a "snobbish father wanting to make a rich marriage for his son" in *Serena Blandish*. The father's pathetic but insidious strategem collapses when Serena proposes at one point to marry his son instead of a more advantageous prospect such as the centenarian Sir Everard Pyncheon or the lecherous Lord Ivor Cream, who has "humbled [tumbled?] every daughter in society." In spite of the earnest discussions of marriage and money, the play tends to become somewhat indecisive and glib. Beneath the preposterous social glitter, however, Behrman makes much more of the hideous spectacle of greed than before. So intent upon their own lives and their own desires are the characters that they believe themselves to be the true center of the universe.

The last of Behrman's ante-Depression plays, *Serena Blandish* opened at the Morosco on February 4, 1929, with Jed Harris the producer. The run consisted of ninety-three performances. It was not a success. "At the time I wrote 'Serena Blandish,' " Behrman once said, "I was far too inexperienced to see the enormous, insurmountable difficulties that the play presented. The Guild, far shrewder, did see them, and rejected it. Jed Harris, in the full tide of success, could not imagine that anything he did would fail."[6]

III   Meteor

In Martin's misreading of Serena's personality and temperament, the "snobbish father" remarks in act II, scene 5 that "she lacks the instinct for *success.*" Behrman's *Meteor* (original title: *The Terrible Gift*) bore down upon the American myth of success more forcefully than any of the other plays, but the theme of the individual's need for economic and social success continued to be a concern in the plays yet to be written. *Meteor,* more so than any of the other plays, tended to mirror the materialistic emphasis of the times, something that *The Second Man* and *Serena Blandish* had not done; and its opening on December 2, 1929, with the Lunts at the Guild followed the stock-market crash of the previous October.

Once more, Behrman had written in *Meteor* a play with rather clear autobiographical overtones. His subject this time was the meteoric rise and fall of a man who calls himself "Raphael Lord" and who is a promising university student with a shadowy past that includes a prison record. Lord, who believes fervently that he can see into the future, rejects an academic career only to win and lose a fortune as a result of his crooked oil speculation in South America. He not only loses his business, but his wife as well. Like Behrman, and like the characters in Behrman's early attempts at naturalistic fiction, Lord is portrayed as a self-made man who is eager to overcome the apparently deprived circumstances under which he grew up; indeed, Behrman thought of him as having " 'ghetto' vitality."[7] In act II, Lord replies angrily to charges of having been ruthless in his rise to power with "Do you know what hunger is?" "What poverty is? What tenement crowding is? What frustration is?" Echoing Behrman's own experience, Lord rejects the opportunity of "teaching in some freshwater college out West"; he prefers instead to take his chances in New York—a preference that had been a part of the early Behrman story "Rupert Goes on the Loose." Unlike Behrman, however, Lord's insatiable passion for success motivates him to stop at nothing in the realization of his ambitions.

Raphael Lord, for all his innate genius, evidently represented what Daniel Asher had been: an example of the misapplication of superior intellectual talent. In spite of Lord's superiority complex, he is, in fact, unusually endowed with mental ability. Behrman describes him as "febrile, restless, [with a brain that] animates him [like] an incessant gyroscope. . . ." His egomania and brashness prefigure the character of Richard Kurt, the young journalist in *Biography.* Unlike Kurt however, Raphael Lord is so convinced of his superiority that he claims that he feels "like God," which he describes as a "marvellous sensation." His exploitation of the Republic of Ariandos for private gain causes him to look very much like a Fascist dictator who, in the words of his wife Anne, seeks to build a Utopia "founded on machine-guns." A later play, *Dunnigan's Daughter* (1945), also concentrates on the money-hungry adventurer who exploits a foreign country for his own economic aggrandizement.

Meteor, of course, reintroduces some of the political opinions and tendencies that had lain dormant in Behrman's writing since the days when he had published leftist fiction. It warns that true "gluttony of power" can bring murder, political tyranny, economic chicanery, control of the press, and suppression of free speech. Lord even contemplates the creation of "The Raphael Lord University." In spite of having had his financial empire exposed and ruined, he ends the play on the telephone; he is preparing to bail himself out of trouble by crushing his adversaries.

The opening scene of *Meteor* occurs "in a small University town in Massachusetts," one which Behrman had undoubtedly created partly from his remembrance of Worcester. The psychology professor Dr. Avery seems clearly patterned after G. Stanley Hall under whom Behrman had studied at Clark College. Lord, while he resembles Behrman in certain respects, seems also to suggest Asher, whose considerable intelligence and astonishing self-confidence Behrman had once found highly impressive. Just as Asher had advised Behrman to abandon plans for a career in acadème, Lord gives the same advice to Douglas Carr, the plodding, hopeful, doctoral candidate.

Meteor is no different from *The Second Man* and from *Serena Blandish* insofar as its chief concern is with success and the acquisition of money; moreover, marriage also plays an important part, for Lord's oil speculations had involved the investment of capital obtained from his brother-in-law Douglas. As the play ends, Lord realizes that he has exploited the economic possibilities of his marriage; and he advises his wife that he no longer needs her. *Meteor* becomes, consequently, an exposure of the senseless, headlong quest after wealth that had especially characterized the years leading up to the Depression. If *The Second Man* and *Serena Blandish* had been smartly removed from the workaday concerns of ordinary people, *Meteor* was far more in touch with the times.

IV   Brief Moment

Brief Moment, which continued for a creditable one hundred and twenty-nine performances at the Belasco Theatre beginning on November 9, 1931, invites comparison with *The Second Man* and with *Serena Blandish*. Again, the marriage question figures prominently; and, as in *Serena Blandish*, Behrman constructed a play around an attractive, intelligent, but déclassée young woman and her chances in the matrimonial marketplace. *Brief Moment* concerns the marriage of Abby Fane, a Blues singer at the Hotsy Totsy club, to the wealthy but ineffective Roderick Dean. Like Serena, Abby undergoes positive change during the play. Although she, too, is socially disadvantaged, she more than compensates for her paucity of polite manners by her diligent social and intellectual efforts, and she learns quickly. Before the play is over, in fact, she is able to offer a little social advice to Roderick's sister Kay.

In *Brief Moment*, Behrman came close to recapturing the light, witty, quick sense of subtle humor that had succeeded so well for him in *The Second Man*. In one particular verbal exchange in the first act between Kay, Roderick, and Harold Sigrift, Roderick announces that he is giving up songwriting:

SIGRIFT: I'm glad you're giving it up, Rod. Rich people should patronize art—when it amuses them—not practice it.
KAY: Oh, why should the poor have all the fun?
RODERICK: Because they have all the talent.
SIGRIFT: Like hell they have. Look at the Cavalier poets.
RODERICK: Look at Shakespeare.
SIGRIFT: You look at him. Shakespeare bores me.

But, as can be expected in a Behrman play, very little overt action occurs. The central emphasis is again upon the complex relationship between money and marriage, and the bulk of the dialogue relates to this central problem. In this play a woman of low social standing but high personal potentiality marries a man of high rank and low potentiality—precisely the opposite marital combination from that which nearly occurs in *The Second Man* between Clark Storey and Kendall Frayne. Like Serena Blandish, Abby is another modern Cinderella—a woman who succeeds in the world because of her pleasing manner and her quick mind. Abby is equipped at one point in the play with a list of words she must not utter if she is to be socially accepted by her husband's friends. In many ways she is similar to the character Kendall Frayne: both are capable, mature women who know the technique of shaping their own destinies while managing their men.

Of Roderick and Abby, Roderick is clearly the weaker of the two. He shares with Clark Storey the knowledge that his insecurity arises from his innate inferiority. "Who the hell am I," he asks. "A millionaire's son. Well what of it! The town's lousy with them. I've been a failure at everything. . ." In *Brief Moment*, Behrman also presents evidence of discord between father and son, a dilemma that he uses again and again. Roderick complains to Abby that his father had been "an overbearing man who impressed it on me early in life that I must justify my existence." But, beyond the father-son conflicts that occur in the plays, Behrman also demonstrates the general friction between generations that he had illustrated in his early writing.

Brief Moment also introduces Behrman's first important Marxist character, the Russian motion-picture director Sergei Voloschyn, who reveals his strong, visceral feeling for what he terms the "proletariat rampant." Politics, like incompatibility between generations, figures in Behrman's next two plays, *Biography* and *End of Summer*. Political questions in turn focus on the problems that result from a deficiency of tolerance between persons of conflicting views.

Roderick, who plays the saxophone tolerably well, in *Brief Moment* becomes the second to Clark Storey in a long line of second-rate artists that haunt Behrman's plays. The socioeconomic differences that separate Abby and Roderick are recreated in later plays, especially in *The Talley Method* (1941) in which a son deliberately irks his eminently "successful" father by marrying beneath himself. The scene of the play is also typical: a glamorous roof apartment more than thirty floors from the ground faces the East River.

Although the play contains the comic figure of the gangster Manny Walsh, Behrman as usual avoids any treatment of "low life." In act I, Roderick makes a telling comment about Manny. Abby has said that Manny has probably "pulled some pretty raw deals to get where he is," and Roderick replies that he gets "hope from the fact that this is a strong man." Manny thus becomes the first of Behrman's many "strong" men: he prevails in life because, like Raphael Lord in *Meteor*, he possesses an almost abnormal determination to succeed. Manny, who regards himself as a strong man, seems to suggest that in his character he is a combination of tyrant and bully.

V   *Biography*

On December 12, 1932, the Theatre Guild produced Behrman's *Biography* at the Guild Theatre. Owing partly to Ina Claire's performance in the role of Marion Froude, the play continued for some two hundred and nineteen performances. The writing of *Biography* began with the aid of a railway stenographer while Behrman was on a train bound for California. He had long thought about writing a play about "a successful portrait painter who had got some of the most famous people in Europe to sit for her—statesmen, composers, archbishops."[8] The portrait painter in *Biography*, Marion Froude, is another of Behrman's "second-rate" artistic talents; but her career has taken her to Russia where she has painted some of the "leading Communists," including Lenin himself.

The action of the play is comparatively simple. At the beginning, Marion is prevailed upon by the young and abrasive proletarian magazine editor Richard Kurt to write her autobiography for serialized publication in *Every Week*. After accepting Kurt's offer, she is approached by her old flame Leander "Bunny" Nolan and by Nolan's prospective father-in-law Orrin Kinnicott, a wealthy and intensely conservative health faddist. Nolan and Kinnicott fear that the disclosure of Marion's supposedly lurid past will expose Nolan as her former lover and thereby destroy his chances of being elected to the United States Senate from Tennessee. Marion, another of the long line of Behrman's emancipated, tolerant women, has not the slightest intention of exposing anyone. But, before the play ends, she has destroyed the harmless but valuable manuscript that she would have submitted to Kurt.

As Behrman had done in *The Second Man*, he concentrates upon personality opposites in *Biography*. Marion Froude and the innocent Slade Kinnicott (Bunny Nolan's betrothed) have much the same maturity-immaturity contrast that Kendall Frayne and Monica Grey display in *The Second Man*. Richard Kurt, the brash, idealistic social reformer, contrasts vividly with both Nolan and Kinnicott. In *Biography*, however, much more is at stake than the complications arising from money and marriage, for the issues center around politics and morality as well as the menace of unbridled ambition that had occupied Behrman's thoughts in *Meteor*. The rhetoric of *Biography* is far less flippant and playful than it had been in *The Second Man* and in *Serena Blandish*: it is increasingly pointed, honest, and direct. The earlier smart, drawing-room glibness has now given way to a more serious, unflinching confrontation with the pressing issues of the day. For example, Marion specifically tells Bunny Nolan in act I that, although "one gets into an idiom that passes for banter," she is being anything but flippant in her conversations with him. With this much settled, she goes to the political heart of the matter by asking him how he sees himself—as Napoleon, as Scipio, or as Mussolini.

As usual, problems developing from money and marriage still play a part, albeit a minor one. Bunny Nolan's candidacy for the Senate depends upon his marriage to Slade Kinnicott and upon the economic support that his prospective father-in-law will provide. Marriage for love is just as clearly impossible as it had been in each of the previous plays. Nolan, interested primarily in his own economic and political success, must feather his nest, and he is willing to marry and become the political dupe of his conservative, southern, newspaper-owner father-in-law.

Read as a political allegory, the play introduces two ultraconservative politicians (Nolan and Kinnicott) who contrast to a young radical (Kurt). Just as Orrin Kinnicott prefigures Hobart Eldridge in *Rain from Heaven* (1934), Richard Kurt himself prefigures the character of Dennis McCarthy in *End of Summer* (1936), although Kurt is a much more fully developed character. Between such ideological extremes is Marion Froude, the tolerant, civilized, freethinking, experienced, wise woman who champions the liberal way—the *via media* between the unworkable extremes of radicalism on one side and conservatism on the other. Neither literally nor symbolically can she form any attachments to either Kurt or Nolan, both of whom she finds conveniently at her disposal. Like her predecessors Kendall Frayne and Serena Blandish, she finally goes her own way: Marion rejects both the hot-blooded reformer and the ultraconservative fanatic.

Marion continually stresses the necessity for maintaining an open, civilized, humanistic point of view. She tells Nolan very frankly in the first act that "you're evil because you're intolerant." But the firebrand leftist reformer Kurt is every bit the menace that Nolan and Kinnicott are, and Marion views Kurt as the kind of potential dictator that Anne Carr had seen in Raphael Lord. Near the close of *Biography*, Kurt lashes at Marion: "Why does the injustice and cruelty go on—year after year—century after century—without change—because—as they grow older—people become *tolerant*! Things amuse them. I hate you and I hate your tolerance. I always did."

The political pattern established in *Biography*, the confrontation of left and right with the moderate liberal voice in the center, characterizes many of Behrman's subsequent plays. Undoubtedly, Marion Froude speaks for the playwright himself by constantly asserting that the polarization of political opinion is best neutralized by tolerant understanding and by rational accommodation. Never a believer in political Utopias, Behrman argues that political questions can be resolved by combining what is possible with what is humane and benevolent.

VI   Rain from Heaven

The Broadway run of *Rain from Heaven* began at the Golden Theatre on Christmas Eve, 1934, and it remained for ninety-nine performances. The title apparently derives from the story of Noah (Genesis, 8:2): "The fountains also of the deep and the windows of heaven were stopped, and the rain from heaven was restrained." The background of the play, however, was Gerhart Hauptmann's rejection of his follower Alfred Kerr, the critic, because of Kerr's failure to endorse the new German nationalism. Although the play reveals its technical and thematic connection to Behrman's earlier successes, the movement of the play is characteristically difficult to recount. *Rain from Heaven* should, in any event, be read primarily as a political allegory much like its predecessor *Biography*.

A group of characters converges in *Rain from Heaven* in the living room of a handsome "English country house not far from Brighton" as guests of Lady Lael Wyngate, another of Behrman's wise, tolerant, experienced women. Among those present is the American Hobart Eldridge, a southerner who is not terribly unlike Orrin Kinnicott in *Biography:* a conservative, dictatorial, "strong man," he hopes for a new world order built upon fascism; and this aspiration motivates his visit to England, where he intends to organize and promote an anti-Communist Youth Movement. Hobart Eldridge is in the company of his brother Rand (evidently modeled on Charles

Lindbergh), who has lately returned from a historic expedition into the Antarctic. Rand's presence in England is ostensibly for the purpose of marrying Lael Wyngate. Also present is the sometime music-critic Hugo Willens (modeled on Alfred Kerr), a German refugee who, along with the Austrian composer Melchior Feydak in *Biography,* suggests a variation on the figure of the eternally wandering Jew. Also present is Sasha Barashaev, a Russian-American pianist who differs from Willens in his desire to conceal his Semitic origins; and with him is Nicoli Jurin, for seventeen years a Russian refugee.

For the first time, Behrman addresses himself to the tragic dilemma of Jewishness in the 1930s. His character Willens has served time in a concentration camp for having written a pamphlet entitled *The Last Jew* in response to the new wave of "Aryan standardization" in Europe. Willens explains the essence of his pamphlet to Lael, Hobart, and Rand in act I:

With the extermination of the Jews, the millennium has been promised the people. And with the efficiency of a well-organized machine, the purpose is all but accomplished. They are all dead—but one—the last Jew. He is about to commit suicide when an excited deputation from the All-Highest comes to see him. There has been a meeting in the sanctum of the Minister of Propaganda. This expert and clever man has seen that the surviving Jew is the most valuable man in the Kingdom. He points out to the Council their dilemma. Let this man die and their policy is bankrupt. They are half naked, without an issue, without a programme, without a scapegoat. The Jews are gone and still no millennium. They are in a panic—till finally a committee is dispatched—and the last Jew is given a subsidy to propagate—

As the second act draws to a close, Rand Eldridge's latent anti-Semitism is suddenly revealed: "You dirty Jew!" he cries out. "It's all right," Willens replies; "this makes me feel right at home."

The general thematic thrust of *Rain from Heaven* is not unlike that of *Biography.* Lael Wyngate, like Marion Froude, is the woman of experience—strong, gracious, resolute and tough-minded—who mediates between some very extreme political polarities. Joseph Wood Krutch, an admirer of S. N. Behrman, pointed out in his review of *Rain from Heaven* for *The Nation,* that "as in 'Biography' there can be no doubt where Behrman's sympathies lie. It is safe, I think, that here also the lady [Lael Wyngate] speaks for him. . . ."[9] Her views, like those of Behrman, are consistently sane and civilized. She informs Hugo Willens near the end of the play of her belief "that in the main people are reasonable and corrigible and sweet—fragments of God." When she tells Rand in the final line of the play that "we're all shut behind our little fences," she is identifying the problem that leads to intolerance.

Rain from Heaven ends, as most Behrman plays do, with no definite or concrete solutions to the staggering problems of political polarization and overt racism. As always, the characters drift to their obscure destinies after having had their say. In this play there is, however, much less of the easy, flippant drawing-room banter of the artificially smart variety that had prevailed in *The Second Man* and *Serena Blandish*. Moreover, *Rain from Heaven* is, after *Serena Blandish*, Behrman's second important play to have a setting outside America and in a kind of neutral territory; as a consequence, the cosmopolitan flavor is more pronounced than is customary. The inclusion of Russians, Jews, Britons, Germans, and Americans invites, of course, a broad gamut of outlook and opinion.

Except that the play clearly reflects the dark turmoil of the 1930s, *Rain from Heaven* cannot be considered as an American problem play; it is one which emphasizes the common international peril of growing fascism. Neither is the play particularly comic, for little in its content could suggest a comic vision. Near the opening of act II, Sasha reminds Lael that "it's no joke the way things are going these days," and her reply is in keeping with the general tone of the play: "It was never a joke at any time the way things were going. Was there ever a moment in history when you weren't surrounded by blood and tears?" As in *Biography*, some mildly deprecating observations are included about Hollywood, but the mood of the play remains decidedly bleak.

VII   End of Summer

When *End of Summer* opened at the Guild Theatre on February 17, 1936, for an eventual run of one hundred and fifty-three performances with Ina Claire in the role of Leonie Frothingham, audiences were seeing the essence of *Rain from Heaven* poured into a somewhat different mold. Thematically, both plays lead in the same direction; and, as in a number of other Behrman plays, the dramatic action of *End of Summer* tends to defy an accurate description. The setting this time is the living room of "a Bay Cottage in Northern Maine," the Frothingham estate, a location Behrman liked to refer to as a "masculine Riviera." Once again the playwright stocks his "charmingly furnished room" with an ample array of generally antagonistic personalities, most of whom have appeared in slightly different guises in earlier plays.

Instead of concentrating upon one woman as the unifying center of attention, Behrman provides three; and each one represents a recognizable generation in America's recent past. The oldest is the clever and wise old Mrs. Wyler who rather obviously represents the "old order": American turn-of-the-century capitalism. She herself has progressed steadily from a "shack in Oil City to [a] mansion on Fifth Avenue," having accidentally been nudged on the road to prosperity by the chance appearance of an oil gusher in her own backyard. All luck aside, Mrs. Wyler attributes her rapid social and economic ascendancy to the old reliable American virtues of hard work and self-help. "Our young men didn't moon about," she assures young Will Dexter on the play's opening scene. "They made opportunities for themselves." Symbolically and literally, Mrs. Wyler expires from old age before the play ends.

Mrs. Wyler's daughter, Leonie Frothingham, who does not look her forty years, is introduced in the first act as "slim, girlish, in a young and quivering ecstasy of living and anticipation," and she represents the generation untouched by the Depression. Except for her proclivity toward scatterbrained impracticality and naiveté, Leonie is another Kendall Frayne, Serena Blandish, Abby Fane, Marion Froude and Lael Wyngate rendered over again. Her refreshing "acceptance of people instantly and uncritically at the best of their own valuation" and her generally wholesome approach to life are characteristics given her because of Behrman's tacit approval of them. Leonie, unfortunately, has been well insulated from the destructive effects of the Depression because of her immense wealth; but she is by no means without a social conscience. While the tolerance and womanly grace of Behrman's earlier feminine protagonists is present in Leonie, the sense of experience that Behrman had portrayed in Kendall Frayne, Marion Froude, and Lael Wyngate is conspicuously absent from the character of Leonie Frothingham.

Paula Frothingham, Leonie's nineteen-year-old daughter, represents the generation of young people who came to their majority during the Depression years, but she is representative in only a limited way. She leans toward a certain hopeful, idealistic activism and toward a totally sober and sincere, if naive, desire to work at correcting some of the social dislocations besetting the country. Like her mother, Paula paradoxically finds herself disadvantaged because of her privileged background.

Behind these three women stand six male characters of somewhat different philosophic persuasions who complete the play's background. The most memorable and imposing of these is Dr. Kenneth Rice, a character who is derived from such earlier Behrman characters as Raphael Lord, Orrin Kinnicott, and Hobart Eldridge; but Rice is no reformer. Rice is a Freudian psychoanalyst from New York whose obscure past and whose pride in knowing himself to be "self-made" are especially reminiscent of Raphael Lord in *Meteor*. Calculating and ruthless, Dr. Rice allows nothing to come between him and his goal. He is attracted to both Leonie and her daughter Paula; but Paula exposes Dr. Rice's plot to marry Leonie for her money so that he would have the necessary capital to finance his own sanatorium. Withal, Rice is the exploiter, the sinister "strong man," whose desire to succeed materially submerges all other considerations.

Will Dexter, the young Amherst student who contemplates the publication of a magazine devoted to the formation of a new, radicalized youth movement, has precisely the opposite political leanings of Hobart Eldridge in *Rain from Heaven*, who hopes to create his own fascist-inspired youth movement. Will Dexter, one of Behrman's uncharacteristically likable young people, is an attractive, principled, forthright, and honest reformer whose inexperience and youthful idealism act to his disadvantage. His partner in the publishing venture is Dennis McCarthy, a parasitic youth of Will's age, whose abrasiveness and brashness recall the character of Richard Kurt in *Biography*. McCarthy, unable to find work because of the Depression, is not only a Roman Catholic partisan but a more politically radical character than Will Dexter with whom he lounges about the Frothingham summer estate.

Will's father, Dr. Dexter, who appears briefly, complains that he has lost his job as a research physicist for being overcompetent. Dr. Dexter is in some respects like Austin Lowe in *The Second Man*; both are frustrated scientific purists who contrast with the more artistic temperaments in their midst. Indeed, scientists do not, as a rule, win Behrman's enthusiastic endorsement. In *End of Summer*, both doctors—Rice and Dexter—are living contradictions of Mrs.

Wyler's view that individual initiative and sustained hard work are the keys to prosperity. Rice, the irrepressible, self-serving fortune hunter, fails to do any better than Dexter, who is understandably cynical and bitter because of his knowledge that his sophisticated scientific learning is not marketable in America.

The other two male characters, Sam Frothingham and Boris, Count Mirsky (another of Behrman's Russians), contribute little to the development of the play. Sam, who speaks with unusual caution, is Paula's father and Leonie's ex-husband. He intends to marry Selena Bryant, a character who never appears. Although divorced, Sam is by no means emotionally unattached to Leonie and Paula, as is evidenced by his continued presence. Count Mirsky, whose aristocratic aura attracts Leonie's attention, is ridden with distressing emotional problems brought about by an unsatisfactory relationship with his father, as Dr. Rice boldly diagnoses.

End of Summer is a kind of Chekovian play which emphasizes the disappearance (or demise) of an old, conservative order and the emergence of the new, more radical way of American life. But, once again, very little is settled when the play ends. Mrs. Wyler and her ways have died, and the destiny of the country may be, by all appearances, in the hands of the younger, idealistic, radical activists who have grown up in the midst of the Depression and who are determined to change the whole structure of American life.

Of course, money and marriage are treated at some length; but this time an important difference occurs: money prevents marriage rather than promotes it. In the second act, Paula tells Will that "it's childish to let an artificial barrier like [money] stand between us. It's also childish to ignore it." Will, however, is unable to reconcile being potentially wealthy on one hand, while devoting his "energies to the poor and downtrodden" on the other. Money also prevents the union of Leonie and Dr. Rice because he is more in love with her money than with her.

One of the unusual aspects of this Depression play is that Behrman chooses to view the problem from the top of the money pyramid. In this play—which is, in respect to point of view, very much unlike *Serena Blandish*—the wealthy are inclined to feel self-conscious about their affluence since the time is one of dire financial crisis for most people. In the first act, Leonie comments that "we who are in the embarrassing position nowadays of being rich must do something with our money, mustn't we?" Her comment explains

in part the otherwise unlikely bargain she strikes at the play's conclusion when she ironically agrees to help finance the very forces
that threaten the traditional American economic system. In the closing line, Dennis comically reassures her that, by backing the new
undergraduate magazine, she will "have a friend in high office"
when the revolution occurs.

Critical reaction to *End of Summer* is interesting not only for the
light it focuses on the play, but for what it says of Behrman the
playwright in general. As Grenville Vernon's review of *End of
Summer* in *The Commonweal* argued, "the real weakness of Mr.
Behrman is that he does not tie together the actions of his characters
in a definite, firm enough pattern; in short, his plays lack form."[10]
Although *End of Summer* survives today as one of Behrman's better
plays, Vernon's criticism applies to it as well as to a number of the
other plays; for Behrman too often succumbed to the temptation of
creating too many characters engaged in what seem to be too many
unrelated quests. The result is that characters seem to be discon-
nected from one another, and from the major thematic intents of the
play.

There are, of course, some very funny lines, some of which originate with Dr. Rice, an otherwise very unfunny character. In the first
act, he inquires of the Irishman Dennis McCarthy whether he "ever
heard of Bismark's solution to the Irish problem." When Leonie
chimes in, "Please tell us. I adore irrelevancies," Rice continues;
"he thought the Irish and the Dutch should exchange countries. The
Dutch, he thought, would very soon make a garden out of Ireland,
and the Irish would forget to mend the dikes." The underlying
issues of Depression life, the changing character of the whole
American experience, and the real possibilities of a new political
and social order are significant, if underplayed. As always, the
civilized virtues of good manners, social grace, tolerance, compassion, and good sense are earnestly recommended. There is a clear
indication in *End of Summer* that change is necessary and desirable,
but the message is also clear that extreme political positions can
never work because they are too severe to succeed. The play calls
for a progressive, positive approach to social change—one that rejects both the conservative and the radical positions. In other words,
Behrman recommends the *via media*: a liberal, humanistic approach
to remedy economic and social problems. Moreover, Behrman uses
the play's movement, from spring to summer to autumn, to under-

line the fact that change is in the air. Even the naive Leonie finally realizes that the traditional American ideals and values she had grown up with need to be reassessed. "It's the end—the end of summer," she gravely reminds her daughter Paula in the play's final act.

CHAPTER 4

The Drama in Decline

A FTER 1936, Behrman saw, with widely varying results, thirteen more of his plays produced on the New York stage. With the exception of *Fanny*, which was an enormous popular triumph as a musical comedy, and *The Cold Wind and the Warm*, which was a regretably unheralded achievement in theatrical artistry, the remaining plays deservedly received mixed reaction from the critics. As a playwright, Behrman gradually curtailed his once vigorous output of plays. In the 1930s, he had enjoyed at least seven satisfactory plays on Broadway; and in the 1940s he prepared five additional ones. There were three more plays in the 1950s and two more in the 1960s, but the decline in their quality and quantity signaled, among other things, that Behrman was turning increasingly toward nondramatic writing: he was nurturing even more his flair for the prose essay.

End of Summer was also in a sense the end of Behrman's fully sustained period of playwriting. The plays extending from *The Second Man* through *End of Summer* seem to have been written in a single burst of continuous, well-rewarded artistic enthusiasm, with variations upon essentially the same fundamental subjects, themes, and dramatic techniques. While the plays beginning with *Amphitryon 38* (1937) do not break with the plays that came before them, they became increasingly uneven in audience appeal and in aesthetic quality.

I Amphitryon 38, Wine of Choice, No Time for Comedy,
The Talley Method

"In a sense," Behrman wrote recently, "most of my playwriting life [beginning especially in 1937] was devoted to Alfred Lunt and Lynn Fontanne, although after my first play, 'The Second Man,' I had only one success with them—the adaptation, which they commissioned me to do, of Jean Giraudoux's 'Amphitryon 38.' "[1] This play, it seems, was developed over a great deal of time and space. "We rehearsed 'Amphitryon 38' in Chicago, in Baltimore, in Boston, in Genesee Depot, and in London, where the Lunts took the playwright Edward Knoblock's house in Cadogan Square for the summer."[2] After its San Francisco tryout, the play opened in New York at the Schubert on November 2, 1937; and it received generally good reviews.

Behrman's not unskillful rendering of Giraudoux's French theatrical success of the same title was what the Frenchman alleged to be the thirty-eighth version of the original Greek myth. Undoubtedly the "38" also conveniently alluded to the tailoring of the myth for a post-modern (1938) audience. It is difficult to separate the Behrman from the Giraudoux contributions, and credit for the witty nuances of plot and structure is partly due to the playwrights who had used the myth before: Plautus, Molière, Dryden. Moreover, Behrman had at least looked at the English translation of *Amphitryon 38* prepared by Aline Caro-De Vaille;[3] but the rhetoric of the play, with its crisp, epigrammatic smartness, seems surely to have been Behrman's.

Amphitryon 38 is essentially a bedroom farce which deals with overt sexuality far more than any Behrman play except his last, *But for Whom Charlie* (1964). Jupiter, with his half-son Mercury, descends to earth with the intention of seducing the delicious but faithful Alkmena whose husband Amphitryon has been sent away by Jupiter to wage a war. Disguised as Amphitryon, Jupiter eventually gains admittance to Alkmena's bedroom and wins his objective. In the end, however, Alkmena and Amphitryon are reunited as husband and wife, and Alkmena persuades Jupiter to regard her as his friend, not as his mistress. Although Alkmena is by this time carrying the as yet unborn Hercules within her, a kiss from Jupiter conveniently erases all recollection of her paradoxically innocent infidelity. Having forgotten all, Alkmena bids Jupiter farewell as he returns to the heavens.

Although the fundamental idea for the play was not Behrman's own, certain subjects, such as the problem of promiscuity, had been touched upon lightly in *The Second Man, Serena Blandish, Brief Moment,* and *Biography;* and marriage in *Amphitryon 38* is treated in much the same way as it had been in the previous plays. In spite of Jupiter's promises of immortality for Alkmena if she will go with him, no bargain is finally struck between them; and Jupiter returns to his celestial dwelling still unattached. The antiwar sentiment which Behrman had partly inherited from Giraudoux clearly pertains to the darkening threat of American involvement in another global war. A warrior runs on stage in the first act to promote with great enthusiasm an all-out conflict between Athens and Thebes. He argues that war has an irresistible appeal to youth, and in so doing he restates some of the same sentiments expressed in *Rain from Heaven*: "You zealots, you prayerful ones, make Nationalism your religion. And you atheists and sensualists, war is your paradise for it legalizes all your excesses—you may whet your swords on the statues of the gods themselves. You who hate to work—to the trenches—war is the haven of the lazy. . . ."

Other than lightly veiled contemporary remarks such as this, relatively little is to be taken seriously in *Amphitryon 38*. Behrman himself, who liked the play very much, called it "an ideal comedy."[4] The play was designed around the Lunts, as *The Pirate* (1942) and *I Know My Love* (1949) were to be later. The center of attention, quite possibly, was more the players than the play. At least one critic, George Freedly, found the play's prologue "scandalously amusing due to the construction of the clouds in Lee Simonson's design making Jupiter and Mercury appear to be reclining barebottomed."[5] The Lunts, however, were at their best. Maurice Zolotow, upon seeing the play, found Lynn Fontanne's performance "a thing that actually shimmered on stage."[6] Behrman's Hollywood days had taught him, among other things, that the "star system" that had succeeded so well in the movies worked as well on the stage.

In contrast to the successful *Amphitryon 38*, Behrman's *Wine of Choice*, which made its New York debut on February 21, 1938, merits very little serious attention. A box-office failure, the play closed at the Guild Theatre after forty-three performances. The trouble had begun in Chicago, where it was first put on stage; for the actors had been apprehensive, even unhappy, about their parts. As a result, Behrman had worked diligently to rectify the play's inherent problems by extensive, overnight rewrites. If some of the earlier Behrman plays are virtually plotless, *Wine of Choice* is static. Needlessly cluttered with irrelevant verbal exchanges, the play seems to lead nowhere and to say very little.

In its conception, the play is not so different from *Biography*, *Rain from Heaven*, and *End of Summer*: a group of guests assemble on the Long Island estate of wealthy Laddy Sears; and there they exchange views about politics, love, marriage, and money. Again, the central female figure in the play is an aspiring woman—film star Wilda Doran who must make a matrimonial choice between her host Laddy Sears and the newspaper-publisher-turned-United-States senator, Ryder Gerrard. Predictably enough, she rejects both prospects.

Among the guests is the young revolutionary writer Dow Christophsen, who bears an obvious resemblance to Raphael Lord (*Meteor*) and Richard Kurt (*Biography*), among others. Dow and Wilda are alike in their desire to nurture an artistic career; but, aside from that, there is little to attract either to the other. Dow is so frighteningly self-assured that he feels himself above reproach; and Behrman, in his preface to the Random House edition of the play, remarks about Dow that what interested him most was "a condition of mind so strained of any element of doubt that opposition or disagreement is converted automatically into either insanity or perversion." The phenomenon of the closed mind had long interested Behrman; and, as has been observed before, his fully humane characters—those like Dr. Avery, Marion Froude, Lael Wyngate—are always those who maintain the proper balance of toleration in their views, particularly in their moral and political ones.

Wine of Choice fares poorly when pitted against some of his better plays of the 1930s. Wilda has not the charm and appeal of Behrman's other emancipated women, because she lacks the wit as well as a quick, creative intelligence. The leftist youth Dow Christophsen is similarly not so fully realized as a character. Although this play is a political one, the positions of the other characters—Charles Dow Hanlon, Binkie Niebuhr, Ryder Gerrard and Leo Traub—are never made clear. *Wine of Choice* contains at least two Jewish characters, Niebuhr and Traub; but the significance of their Jewishness in the context of the play is, again, indefinite. As in *Rain from Heaven*, in which Hugo Willens relates the allegory of "The Last Jew," a similar anecdote is told when, toward the end of the second act, Binkie relates a story involving the military governor of the Lithuanian town in which he was born:

One day I invited the governor to our hovel to taste some special dishes— you see my sainted mother was a superb ethnic cook. The great man came, ate his fill and was delighted. There were six of us—my mother, and my

little brothers and sisters. As I saw him to the door he put his hand in the
pocket of his greatcoat and took out six rosettes. "Here," he said. "Enough
for the whole family. Wear them—wear them. . . . There's been so much un-
rest," he said, "among the unemployed factory workers, that I've ordered a
pogrom for tomorrow—do the lads good to let off a little steam. By tomorrow night the Jewish population of Chupolpic will be considerably reduced.
But I am giving orders that those wearing rosettes will be immune. . . .

Needless to say, such is not the stuff of comedy; but Behrman's
concern for the destiny of contemporary Jewry is present in this play
as it had been in *Biography* and in *Rain from Heaven*. Curiously
enough, however, Binkie's anecdote evinces only puzzling re-
sponses from his listeners. Says Traub, "your mother must have
been an awful good cook." Laddy Sears, somewhat more moved,
comments, "I wish I could locate the governor who did me the
service of sparing Binkie, and reward him personally. . . . Here,
Binkie, a rosette for you." Behrman's other treatments of Jewish life
and culture appears in two later plays, *Jacobowsky and the Colonel*
and *The Cold Wind and the Warm*. In four of his prose works, *The
Worcester Account, Duveen, The Burning Glass* and *People in a
Diary*, he devotes also considerable time and space to the matter of
Jewishness.

No Time for Comedy (performed one hundred and eighty-five
times, beginning April 17, 1939, at the Ethel Barrymore) is not
concerned with Jewish life but with the comic vision of life. An
understanding of the play is necessary for an understanding of
Behrman. It centers around an established writer of comedies
(Gaylord Esterbrook) who is currently troubled by being "between
ideas"—in a state of limbo, he is waiting nervously for the necessary
inspiration to write a new play. Whether this situation necessarily
contains any autobiographical overtones is conjectural; but in any
case, "Gay" has fallen under the spell of Amanda Smith, the attractive wife of a banker. She has convinced Gay that his next play
should spurn comedy and turn to a darker, more tragic vision of
life—one that would seem, after all, more appropriate for the times.
Gay's wife Linda, a successful actress who depends upon her husband for good comedy scripts, is also anxiously awaiting another
play. In the meantime, a romantic attachment forms between Gay
and Amanda; and Gay threatens for a time to divorce Linda. At the
end of the play, Linda confronts Gay with a solution both to his

marital problems and to his lack of inspiration. She suggests that he write about herself and Amanda: "two types of women in the life of a man, an artist, a writer—the builder-upper and the breaker-downer—the critical faculty versus the clinging vine. What Every Woman Knows in reverse."

The opening scene and some of the characters are in the Behrman tradition: "the livingroom of a tower-apartment on the forty-second floor of a smart New York hotel." Linda herself is another added to the long list of those women who possess intelligence and the mature capability to shape their own destinies while they deal effectively with the weak men in their lives. The strong-woman weak-man pattern had been part of the dramatic structure of *The Second Man*, *Serena Blandish*, *Brief Moment*, *Rain from Heaven*, and *End of Summer*. Although Gay is not the second-rate writer that Clark Storey was, he is still the creative, artistic personality who is caught in a non-productive period. The potential for matrimonial indiscretion in this play is equal to that of *Amphitryon 38*, except that, when all is said and done, no one has significantly misbehaved. The discord between sons and fathers (or father surrogates) that had been present in *Serena Blandish*, *Brief Moment*, and *End of Summer* also figures in this play: Philo Smith, Amanda's husband, who in the first act admits to being "desperately" afraid of his own son, a Harvard senior, is in turn accused by the son of being at "the top in an evil system." In the following act, Amanda explains to Linda that Philo has himself "always been obsessed by the fear of never being able to surpass his father."

For once, however, money is not a source of contention; indeed, Behrman's characters are by this time too comfortably established to worry about dollars. The play's real emphasis is on the role of comedy in a tragic world—a world in which the comedic writer can contribute his necessary vision of the human condition. When Gay is finally convinced to do as his wife Linda has urged—"cultivate your garden"—he denies his desire to compose an agonized picture of the times that he has intended to call "Dilemma." He elects, instead, to write a comedy to be titled, with a note of irony, "No Time for Comedy." The central problem in Behrman's play, as Joseph Wood Krutch has correctly identified it, is "a comic writer living in an age which focuses his attention upon conflicts which the comic spirit seems incapable of resolving."[7] In *No Time for Comedy*, at least, Behrman offered something more concrete and conclusive; the play's final scene, which Behrman rewrote eight times, shows Gay about to write his comic play, but on Linda's terms.

Behrman's next play, *The Talley Method* (1941), seemingly indicates that Behrman himself had very little time for comedy, since there is precious little of it in the script. The play, dedicated to his friend Robert Sherwood, heralded the return of Ina Claire to a Behrman production, although even she could not generate more than fifty-six performances, beginning on February 14, 1941, at Henry Miller's Theatre. The limited success of the play was perhaps surprising at the time, because *The Talley Method* contains a little of everything that Behrman had written with success previously. For example, the hub of the play's action is a fully mature, fully humanized woman, and the other characters revolve around her. This woman is Ina Claire in the role of Enid Fuller. At the beginning of the play Miss Fuller intends to marry the widower Dr. Axton Talley, a celebrated New York surgeon, a character who was evidently modeled on Behrman's eccentric physician friend Dr. Emanuel Libman. Dr. Talley has devoted his full energies to the development of the "Talley Method," a uniquely successful (if unexplained) approach to surgery. Although Talley takes extraordinarily good care of his patients, and although he conscientiously labors for satisfactions beyond material wealth, he has become a monomaniac with regard to his medical interests. As a consequence, he has lost rapport with virtually everyone, especially with his son Philip and his adopted daugher Avis. Like Dr. Kenneth Rice in *End of Summer*, Talley is adamant and dictatorial; and, as Wolcott Gibbs observed, Talley is "an almost perfect symbol of enlightened dictatorship."[8] Enid Fuller, however, exhibits almost the opposite characteristics; and Brooks Atkinson correctly described her in his review as "the plastic mind that embraces everything it meets and the imagination that goes out instinctively to suffering and bewilderment."[9]

Talley's son Philip, who has "flunked" medical school, intends to marry a Greenwich Village stripper as an evidently intentional act of defiance against his father's social and professional respectability. Like Roderick Dean in *Brief Moment*, Philip harbors strong antagonism toward his father, as well as a feeling of his own general inadequacy. Dr. Talley, like the snobbish father Martin in *Serena Blandish*, wishes a rich marriage for his son; but it is not to be. Avis Talley, Philip's sister, not only recalls the character of Joan Eldridge in *Rain from Heaven* but also Paula Frothingham in *End of Summer*. Like Paula, Avis is idealistically involved with a leftist youth congress devoted to precipitating social change. Contrary to her anti-Semitic father's wishes, she intends to marry Manfred Geist, a Jewish refugee-poet who has lately fled Nazi Germany and who, during the course of the play, takes his own life. Cy Blodgett, a perpetual student at Columbia who is also passionately committed to the correction of current social problems in America, looks very much like another example of Behrman's occasional touches of self-portraiture.

As usual, the contemplated marriages fail to materialize. Enid wisely realizes that she and Dr. Talley can never bridge the gulf between them. His intolerance and his closed mind, she comes to realize, are permanent obstacles to their union. As she tells him at the conclusion of the play, "there are destructive forces in the world now of violence and ruthlessness, and I am frightened of these things I find in you which are like those forces. I'm sorry, Axton, but I can't possibly marry you." Once again, the focal character is the wise woman caught, as Marion Froude and Lael Wyngate had been, between some irreconcilable extremes—a youthful, idealistic Marxian in one instance and a Fascist, dictatorial strong man in the other. Enid elects to look after Avis; but, other than that, she has no choice but to leave a puzzled and distraught Dr. Talley to manage for himself as best he can.

II   The Pirate, Jacobowsky and the Colonel, Dunnigan's Daughter

According to Maurice Zolotow, *The Pirate* (1942) was written by Behrman during a visit with the Lunts in their home in Genesee Depot, Wisconsin, at the urging of Alfred Lunt, who "for many years . . . had been asking . . . Behrman to write a frivolous play in which he could do magic tricks and walk a tightrope."[10] Lunt specifically had in mind an adaptation of Ludwig Fulda's *Die Seerauber* (The Sea Robber). In 1917 he had played the role of Trillo in Louis N. Parker's translation of the Fulda play at the Pabst Theatre in Milwaukee, and he evidently wanted the play revived with a fresh translation. After the Theatre Guild had prevailed upon Behrman to do such a translation, his original version had been rejected,[11] but this second version was produced.

The Pirate played one hundred and seventy-seven performances at the Martin Beck Theatre after its opening on November 23, 1942, and it became the most financially rewarding play to date for Behrman. According to Lawrence Langner, the motion-picture rights to the play were negotiated by Harold Freedman for $275,000.[12] Ironically, however, the play's out-of-town reception was so bad that it nearly closed before reaching New York. "'The Pirate' and 'I Know My Love' gave me and them [the Lunts] great trouble," Behrman remarked years later. "My adaptations of these plays didn't stack up."[13]

Not only is there a touch of Fulda in the play, but a little Shake-speare as well; for *The Pirate* in fact, owes, something to *The Tempest*. The play is about an invasion of a small West Indian town by a troupe of entertainers, one of whom woos and wins the leading lady of the play, Manuela. Other details such as the application of magic, the "joyous epithalamium" at the end, and certain character names like Estaban, Trillo, and Manuela remind the playgoer of *The Tempest* with its reliance on magic spells, its matrimonial theme, and its characters Calaban, Trinculo, and Miranda.

Problems involving marital fidelity and mistaken identity are raised in *The Pirate,* just as they had been in *Amphitryon 38;* and Behrman was fortunate in having the Lunts carry the two major roles and become the center of attraction in the play that they had been in *Amphitryon 38.* The dramatic movement, for once, is relatively simple. The play concentrates, in Behrman's words, upon "a world-famous pirate [Estramudo] with an itch for respectability [who] retires to a small community, marries [Manuela] and then becomes the village censor."[14] Manuela, however, believes her husband to be Pedro Vargas, a small-time entrepreneur. Serafin, who heads the band of traveling entertainers, arrives in town and finds himself attracted to Manuela; and, at the same time, he imper-sonates the fabled pirate Estramudo about whom Manuela dreams. Finally, with correct identities established, Pedro is arrested, his marriage to Manuela is dissolved, and his former wife is carried away by Serafin.

Of all the Behrman plays, only *Amphitryon 38, The Pirate,* and *Fanny* escape far into the world of romance; and all three are adapta-tions from foreign sources, which in part explains the heavy use of romantic theme and plot. Like the other two plays, *The Pirate* has little more to offer than entertainment, which may well be sufficient justification. Krutch, in his review of the play, called it "a harmlessly naughty bit of romantic fluff" which was "intended merely to provide an extravagant romp for Mr. Lunt and Miss Fontanne."[15] His assessment of the play is fair enough, but other critics were not so sparing. Louis Kronenberger, among others, found *The Pirate* both dull and confusing: "Call it an extravaganza, an opera bouffe, a vehicle, a period piece, a costume job, a high styled bore, a polished impromptu—anything, indeed, except a play."[16]

Behrman's only topical war play, *Jacobowsky and the Colonel*, made its New York debut at the Martin Beck on March 14, 1944, after having left the Schubert in New Haven. The original play belonged to German novelist and dramatist Franz Werfel, who resided in California at the time of the play's American adaptation. Behrman transformed Werfel's intensely serious, sober drama into a loosely tragicomic play. Not unlike his own character Gay Esterbrook in *No Time for Comedy*, he chose to depict the tragedy of the era through an ironically comic point of view.

What happens in the play is based upon an incident Werfel had heard of in Paris when he himself was attempting to escape the Nazis. "It involved," Behrman recently wrote, "Samuel L. Jocobowsky, a Polish Jewish businessman who in his prosperous days had found time for literature and chamber music. He buys a car from a rascally chauffeur. He can't drive, but he trusts to luck to find somebody who can. An anti-Semitic Polish colonel, a cavalry officer, happens along; he has a military mission to the South of France. The idea of travelling with Jacobowsky revolts him, but he has to get away from the Germans and here is a car. His aide beside him, he takes the wheel. Jacobowsky is allowed to occupy the back seat. To Jacobowsky's horror, instead of heading south the colonel heads north, where the Germans are, to pick up his sweetheart, a French girl."[17]

Jacobowsky is the best example of Behrman's eternally wandering Jew: "I've spent my life in a futile effort to become a citizen of some country," he says in the first act. Resourceful and good-humored, Jacobowsky retains his spirits under the unimaginable pressures of Nazi terrorism that threaten his life. His buoyant character, in fact, stands in high relief against the tragedy that has befallen wartime Europe. Jacobowsky's uncanny ability to bargain and to deal is emphasized later in a similar way in Behrman's portrait of Joseph Duveen, the extraordinary art dealer.

Jacobowsky's words to the colonel in the first act help to fix this play in the context of Behrman's previous work. The Jew proposes that they locate a certain automobile and flee Paris before the Nazis occupy it, but the anti-Semitic colonel replies that he is particular about the company with whom he travels. Jacobowsky then argues that the two of them supplement each other very well: "You are a strong man . . . I am a resourceful man." The French girl Marianne, who is romantically involved with the colonel, appears with the identical problem that Enid Fuller has faced in *The Talley Method:* she finds herself unable to give herself to a man quite so full of intolerance.

The conversation between Jacobowsky and Marianne in the final scene of the play strikes a familiar Behrman note:

JACOBOWSKY: One day you will marry him [the colonel]?
MARIANNE: I'm not sure I'll marry him.
JACOBOWSKY: (probing delicately to touch his fate) But you'll always be in love with him? Of that you are sure?
MARIANNE: (looks at him, wants to tell the complete truth, firmly) Yes. (This is final. Jacobowsky receives the final coup de grace, straightens up.) But until he learns a little of what you know—I cannot marry him.

Except for these important lines, the marriage question is never seriously raised. Marianne is left on the French shore as the colonel and his party prepare to make their way to political exile in England. Marriage, once again, is evaded.

If a conspicuous weakness exists in *Jacobowsky and the Colonel*, it is one that had long plagued Behrman plays: a seemingly irresistible tendency to become structurally diffuse. In each of his plays, a certain amount of dialogue is not organically functional. Stark Young, writing for *The New Republic*, commented that "what we have [in *Jacobowsky and the Colonel*] is neither flesh, fish nor fowl, with whimsy, gush, eloquence, international significance, epigrams, high prophecy and ordinary clichés, all in a plausible wooing wash."[18] Notwithstanding, *Jacobowsky and the Colonel* lasted for four hundred and fifteen performances and was the longest-running Behrman play to this point.

In Behrman's note of acknowledgment to the Random House edition of *Dunnigan's Daughter* (1945), he gave credit to "Mr. Lawrence Duggan, formerly in charge of International Affairs with our State Department in Washington [who] is a known friend of the Mexican people" for the raw materials of his new play.

Dunnigan's Daughter, however, also bore a certain similarity to Katherine Anne Porter's classic short story "Flowering Judas" (1930). Both the play and the story center upon an American woman who lives temporarily in rural Mexico; and both women teach English to Mexican children as a good will gesture. Both are inclined toward revolutionary politics; both are pursued by Marxist seducers with artistic inclinations, and both are haunted by the memory of a political prisoner's suicide.

When the New York cast of *Dunnigan's Daughter* opened the day after Christmas in 1945 at the Golden Theatre, the followers of S. N. Behrman's plays must surely have recognized that the telltale characteristics of his earlier plays were again present. Along with *Meteor* and *The Pirate*, the play is set in a Latin American country; and, like *Meteor* especially, the play deals with the exploitation of foreign resources by an unscrupulous American entrepreneur. And entrepreneur Clay Ranier is a character quite obviously cast in the mold of Behrman's other strong men. The stage notes call for a man "with a dynamism that nothing can down." Toward the conclusion of the second act, Ranier tells his wife Fern (the late Jim Dunnigan's daughter) that he believes himself to be among the "superior few" in whose hands the power in this world rests. At the opening of the third act, he refers to himself as a "strong man."

Fern Dunnigan Ranier is also cast in a familiar Behrman role. Her intelligence and humanism are traceable to such Behrman women as Kendall Frayne, Serena Blandish, Marion Froude, Linda Esterbrook, and Enid Fuller. Fern's stepdaughter Zelda bears the same innocence-experience relationship to Fern that Monica Grey bears to Kendall Frayne in *The Second Man* and that Avis Talley has to Enid Fuller in *The Talley Method*. The Marxist painter Miguel Riachi seems surely to have evolved from a series of Behrman's radical writers and artists such as Richard Kurt and Dow Christophsen—men who, in Behrman's judgment, are ineffective because of their intolerant, overzealous economic and political views.

Fern, like most of her Behrman predecessors, has a critical decision to make; she must either play the role of obedient wife or go her own way in order to follow her humane inclinations. She decides, as Enid Fuller had in *The Talley Method*, that, as long as a choice must be made, the freedom to obey one's social conscience is far more important than endeavoring to live in matrimonial harmony. Finally, Zelda and Fern leave Clay Ranier and join Jim Baird, a youthful state-department representative who is preparing to investigate and expose Ranier's businessman's morality.

As is characteristic of Behrman's other lesser plays, *Dunnigan's Daughter* is needlessly diffuse and involved both in subject matter and in rhetoric. As reviewer Ward Morehouse indicated, "Behrman expounds and sermonizes on social and economic problems. He lets go on the subject of love, matrimony, high finance and the state of the world that lies ahead. His dialogue is glib, literate and frequently amusing but *Dunnigan's Daughter* remains a disorganized conversation piece. It never begins to build into a play."[19] Predictably, the play closed after thirty-eight performances, the shortest run experienced by any Behrman play.

III   I Know My Love, Jane, Fanny

The critics were essentially of one mind about *I Know My Love* after its November 2, 1949, opening at the Schubert in New York. Richard Watts, Jr. of The New York Post found it to be "a sprawling and uncertain play,"[20] and Morehouse's review for *The New York Sun* called it "a pretty flimsy play . . . loose and scattered . . . crowded with subplots . . . crammed with some uninteresting characters."[21] Agreeing with most of her fellow critics, Margaret Marshall viewed Behrman's new comedy as "an exhibition piece arranged for the acting and the acting together of Miss Fontanne and Mr. Lunt,"[22] which it was. Brooks Atkinson accused the play of being "untidy in construction, cluttered with clichés and nonentities. . . ." As for the acting, he continued, "there are a number of scenes in which the Lunts do not appear. That makes for heavy going."[23]

Although *I Know My Love* was an adaptation of Marcel Achard's *Auprès de Ma Blonde*, the style and content of the play seem to be pure Behrman. "The idea behind this play was a very good one," he believed, "—that a very happy married couple arouse envy and hatred in those around them, even within their own families."[24] Behrman's version of the Achard play is an intensely involved chronicle of the courtship and married life of Tom and Emily Chanler, and the narrative begins in Boston on Christmas Day, 1888, and continues until January, 1939. The swift chronological movement obliged the Lunts to undergo four separate makeup changes during each performance, and complications inevitably arose when the play attempted to treat multiple characters from different generations on both sides of the marriage.

A number of early Behrman preoccupations are again present in *I Know My Love*. Both at the beginning and at the end, the characters mull over the influence of money on marriage; and conflict between the generations is given a great deal of emphasis. Tom Chanler appears at the beginning of the play as a young crusader (somewhat in the tradition of Richard Kurt and Dennis McCarthy) who alienates his future father-in-law by writing a newspaper editorial calling for the working day to be reduced to a mere thirteen hours. The father-in-law, a textile tycoon, is the same kind of physical-culture faddist that Orrin Kinnicott had been in *Biography*. Ironically, Tom becomes in old age what his father-in-law had been: a man concerned primarily with questions of profit and loss, temperamentally intolerant and crotchety.

The play mainly concerns marriage, however, and the conclusion toward which the play leads is that, even at best, marriage is not a bed of roses. In the final scene, a reporter who is interviewing old Emily Chanler asks how one makes "a success of marriage." After reflecting about her arduous years as wife, mother, and grandmother, her response is perhaps inevitable: "you rise above it."

Behrman's next play, the Broadway version of *Jane* (1952), did not open until February 1, 1952, at the Coronet; but Behrman had been tinkering with it for at least five years. *Jane*, an adaptation of W. Somerset Maugham's short story of the same title, was a play subjected to many rewrites. Begun in 1946 at the urging of Theresa Helburn of the Theatre Guild, the play was produced originally in Blackpool, England. There, *Jane* opened in the midst of a four-day snowstorm and a coal strike. When low temperatures became too severe, Behrman was obliged to do his rewrites in a hotel bed to keep warm.[25] The play then moved on to London: but, before it finally reached New York, six additional rewrites were necessary for the play to survive its one hundred performances.

In *Jane*, the year is 1937. The scene is Hyde Park Gate, London, and the living room of recently divorced Millicent Tower. The characters who assemble there are typical of earlier Behrman creation. Millicent herself is as hopelessly impractical and scatter-brained as Leonie Frothingham is in *End of Summer*. Millicent's

daughter Ann and her romantic companion, the youthful poet-
journalist Peter Crewe, function as the two romantic leads in the
play in much the same fashion that Paula Frothingham and Will
Dexter do in *End of Summer*. Another of the guests in the household is the lecherous newspaper publisher Lord Frobisher, who is
one more in Behrman's succession of fascist strong men.

The main attraction, however, is Jane Fowler, who is described in
the stage directions as "a vital little middle-aged lady" who gives the
impression of "youth, vitality and clarity of outlook, even
eagerness." Jane astonishes everyone by matter-of-factly announc-
ing her pending marriage to fortune-hunting Gilbert Dabney, a
thirty-year-old interior decorator. Meanwhile, because of her penchant for uttering the truth, Jane becomes the overnight social rage
of London until she tires of socializing. By the play's end, the marriage has failed, as Jane had openly suspected it might; and she finds
herself paired (ironically) with the Lord Frobisher after a complicated deception in which William Tower makes a mock proposal of
marriage to Jane.

The play is scarcely under way before Peter Crewe reveals that he
is married to a woman now detained in a Nazi concentration camp.
Crewe's marriage, undertaken for the purpose of rescuing the im-
prisoned woman, needs to be dissolved before matrimonial plans
between Peter and Ann can be made. Through Frobisher's political
connections, the woman is released by the Nazis; and the major
problems in the play—the imprisonment of an innocent woman, the
legal impediments to the matrimonial plans of Peter and Ann, and
ideological differences that stand between Jane and Frobisher—are
apparently moving toward a solution when the play ends.

In an interview with *The New York Times*, Behrman spoke of his
intentions in *Jane*: "The point I wanted to make in the play is that
youth is a question of vitality, generosity, warmth, and general
sympathy in point of view. A stuffed shirt may be old at 20. Jane is
alive and vital and will be young and vital at 80."[26] Jane's eccentric,
paradoxical behavior, as evidenced by her unlikely attachment first
to Gilbert Dabney and then to Lord Frobisher, perhaps defies rational explanation. Hearing in the final scene that Jane is in love
with Frobisher, Millicent exclaims, "I've never heard of anything so
grotesque, so fantastic, so unbelievable!" In the closing line, Jane
notes that love is not subject to rational explanation; and her attraction to Frobisher "is believable because it is the truth!"

Jane is in many ways a witty and arresting play; but it, too, is marred, like most of Behrman's plays after 1936, by a fundamental lack of structural tightness and coherence. While the play is an improvement over the diffuse *I Know My Love*, it was not enough of one to satisfy critics such as Walter Kerr who argued that *Jane* "stubbornly [refused] to come into focus, and [that] Mr. Behrman's frequently stunning lines [were] left dangling in mid-air." He continued, "if 'Jane' had any clear sense of where it was going from laugh to laugh, it might have made a captivating comedy of manners."²⁷

Behrman's only musical comedy effort, *Fanny*, was written in collaboration with Joshua Logan. With music and lyrics supplied by Harold Rome, *Fanny* was an adaptation of a trilogy of stories and films by Marcel Pagnol. The original New York production of twenty-nine performances opened at the Majestic on November 4, 1954. Along with such plays as *Amphitryon 38, The Pirate*, and *I Know My Love*, *Fanny* was tailored almost exclusively for entertainment value, although it resembles in certain respects Eugene O'Neill's *Beyond the Horizon* (1920) in its rejection of provincial life, its crises imposed by spur-of-the-moment judgments, and its reuniting of long-parted lovers.

Fanny is set in old Marseilles at a time "not so long ago." The primary focus of the play is upon the young lovers Marius ("a boy with no heart to give") and Fanny, the attractive daughter of the fishwife Honorine. The callow Marius is painfully torn between his intense longing for the sea—he desperately wants to accept an offer to make a five-year voyage—and his ardent desire for Fanny. He elects to sail away, but not before he has unknowingly gotten Fanny with child. In the meantime, old Panisse, a wealthy sailmaker who has recently lost his own wife, has been vainly trying to win Fanny's affection. When Honorine discovers her daughter's problem, she easily arranges Fanny's marriage to Panisse, who is delighted with the mere possibility of having the son he had always wanted and who wants to be credited with the child's paternity. An understanding with Marius's father Cesar is worked out, and the child is to be named "Cesar Marius Panisse." After the child's birth, Marius unexpectedly returns from the sea and quickly ascertains the child's real paternity; but having no immediate chance to possess Fanny again, Marius leaves immediately for America. The dilemma of the two lovers is finally solved when Panisse, on his deathbed, magnanimously writes Marius a letter beginning "Dear Marius. This is a proposal of marriage. Will you do me the honor to marry my wife? She will be free soon—." Having unselfishly prepared the way for the reunion of Fanny and Marius, Panisse dies as the final curtain descends.

Despite the combined influence of many individuals who helped shape *Fanny*, a number of identifying Behrman touches exist. The conflict that develops between Marius and his father recalls a similar problem in *Serena Blandish, Brief Moment,* and *The Talley Method.* The marriage of convenience between Fanny and the aging Panisse is one more of the many examples in Behrman's plays where security and money are far more a consideration in marriage than love. The unwanted, accidental pregnancy, moreover, is a problem that Behrman had used in *The Second Man* (when Monica Grey falsely claims to be pregnant), in *Amphitryon 38,* in *I Know My Love,* and in *The Cold Wind and the Warm.* The practice of matrimonial matchmaking is treated in a succession of plays including *The Second Man, Serena Blandish, Wine of Choice, The Talley Method,* and *Jane.* Marius's resistance to narrow provincialism and his desire to see the world first-hand is a minor idea in Behrman's writing that reaches back to his early short stories, especially "Rupert Goes on the Loose." In *Meteor,* Raphael Lord finds (as Marius does) that the quiet, conservative, safe life is intolerable. Withal, *Fanny* is first and last a romantic excursion; and the playgoer is not likely to find himself searching for any particularly imposing themes.

IV   The Cold Wind and the Warm

Behrman's next two plays, *The Cold Wind and the Warm* (1958) and *Lord Pengo* (1962), are derived from his own prose essays. *The Cold Wind and the Warm* is the quintessence of his light, yet emotionally charged series of autobiographical essays written for inclusion in *The New Yorker* which were later collected as *The Worcester Account*; and *Lord Pengo* developed in a similar way from his series about Joseph Duveen in *The New Yorker.* It was unlikely that Behrman, at the age of sixty-five, and after a series of generally mediocre plays written since 1936, would produce a best play in *The Cold Wind and the Warm,* but he did so. Perhaps the quality of the play derived in part from his greater willingness to reveal certain deeply felt elements in his private history.

The Cold Wind and the Warm is a play of remembrance with a poetic quality quite unlike anything Behrman had written before. Relatively plotless, the drama is a montage of scenes from the playwright's past; and these center upon his youth in Worcester, Massachusetts. More than anything, however, it is a haunting remembrance of Daniel Asher ("Willie Lavin") played on the stage by Eli Wallach. Tobey Sacher, a twelve-year-old Jewish boy when the play opens, is Behrman's self-portrait. Tobey's father, a rendering of Joseph Behrman, was played by the distinguished Jewish actor Morris Carnovsky. Behrman's mother, curiously enough, does not appear at all.

The tone of the play is fixed in the opening moments of the first act. The stage is dark; and the voice of Tobey is heard, prompted by "his meditation on a vanished past and particularly [by] the enigma of a lost but still-abiding friendship of his youth. Through the dissolving darkness we hear a lovely plaintive melody: the oboe passage from the second movement of Handel's Water Music." Tobey's first utterance is particularly moving. Approaching the age of sixty, he looks into the dim past:

I find that as I grow older that I keep going back to my friendship with Willie—when we were young and happy and living in Worcester, Massachusetts, in the early years of the century. Willie was always preoccupied with mystery—the mystery of life—the mystery of death. He used to illuminate all my childish problems for me. But he left me an inheritance of the greatest mystery of all: why he killed himself, why he felt he had to do it. What were the steep walls in Willie's mind that converged on him to destroy him? I don't know. What I do know, as I look back on my relationship with him—and on his relationship with others—was that he was the most life-giving person I have ever known. I remember still the first mysteries I brought him to solve: the mystery of infinity, the mystery of the True Name of the Lord. Did Willie, at the end, ponder these mysteries? Had he sought the True Name? Did he, I wonder, come too close? I don't know. I shall never know. I can only tell what I remember.

The structure of the play runs full circle. At the end, Tobey has returned to the place where the play began: the office of Dr. Jim Nightingale, the only non-Jewish character in the play. Nightingale, who is very unsentimental and very realistic about life, listens while Tobey reflects again about the events of the past: "Jim, now that I'm back here, the whole past is like a heavy sack around me. All the dead—my father and mother—Dan [a childhood friend] and Willie—the anonymous dead. (Sits on sofa) What does it all mean

anyway?" The doctor's reply contributes to the unraveling of Tobey's past: "Why does life have to have meaning? It's good in itself. . . . You speak of the anonymous dead. They're not anonymous. They're figures in the tapestry in which we ourselves are
figures. They've given us what we are...."

Although Jews had figured in some of Behrman's earlier plays, no
other drama (with the possible exception of *Jacobowsky and the
Colonel*) had been a strictly Jewish play. In *The Cold Wind and the
Warm*, Behrman uses Jewish characters; and his knowledge of
Jewish life resulted in a thoroughly believable, living drama based
upon his personal past. Portraits of life from among the orthodox
Jewish families in an industrial New England city at the turn of the
century are in themselves good theatrical material. Moreover,
Behrman closes in on a familiar theme: the conflict between the old
(Jewish) orthodoxy (represented by Tobey's father) and a less
tradition-conscious generation (represented by Willie Lavin). However, other Behrman thematic preoccupations—the marriage problems and the quest for material wealth, for education, for
"success"—are present.

Critical reception of the play was mostly negative, but Brooks
Atkinson was one of the critics who recognized its strength. Walter
Kerr applauded it as "a gentle, random, elusively written memory
piece."[28] John Chapman saw it as "an affectionate, frequently
humorous but oddly unresolved play."[29] The unidentified reviewer
in *America*, perhaps recalling some of Behrman's weaker plays,
found that *The Cold Wind and the Warm* "meanders like a contem-
plative novel";[30] and Richard Hayes complained in *The Commonweal* that the play was marred by its "muddiness of focus."[31]

In truth, *The Cold Wind and the Warm*, like so many Behrman
plays before it, was rendered needlessly complicated by the interac-
tion of a dozen characters, some of whom might well have been cut
from the script. In comparison to *The Second Man*, produced thirty
years before, the number of characters was increased threefold; and
the introspective, soulful characters themselves are nothing at all
like the superficially smart company of *The Second Man* and *Serena
Blandish*. Most importantly, Behrman had succeeded in *The Cold
Wind and the Warm* in shedding the strictly external "outer drama"
of superficiality and had replaced it with a compelling "inner drama." Unquestionably, Behrman had composed the finest play of his
career. It lasted for one hundred and twenty performances after it
first opened at the Morosco on December 8, 1958.

V   Lord Pengo, But For Whom Charlie

Unfortunately, Behrman's last two plays returned to the usual mold; but *Lord Pengo,* when first presented in New York at the Royale on November 9, 1962, seemingly appealed to playgoers since it enjoyed a hundred and seventy-five performances. It was what John Chapman found it to be, "a civilized play"[32] with a dash of wit, elegance, and pathos. To followers of Behrman plays, *Lord Pengo* invites comparison with *The Talley Method*; Pengo, inspired by the character of Joseph Duveen, the international art trader, is Behrman's last "strong man" figure; and the similarity between him and Dr. Talley is clear. Supremely self-confident and totally self-assured, Pengo dominates those with whom he comes in contact, be they family or business associations. There is again the bitter conflict between father and son, which comes about as the result of an accomplished, domineering father and a faltering, unaccomplished son who lock horns in the play's central dramatic struggle. Miss Swanson, Pengo's secretary of thirty years, is second from the end in a lengthy succession of Behrman's potentially loving women, such as Enid Fuller in *The Talley Method,* who are driven away by the domineering men to whom they are emotionally attached.

The fascination with high life in *Lord Pengo* is as present as it had been in the plays of the 1930s. The play consists mostly of a number of conversations between Pengo and his clients, many of whom are "successful" but vulgar, newly rich Americans with huge quantities of money to spend. Pengo's business is selling culture at a high price to customers who seem to enjoy paying handsomely for what they receive. Moreover, Pengo has a way of supervising the very lives of his clients not only culturally but (like Bunky Niebuhr in *Wine of Choice*) personally. He arranges marriages and gets accommodations on fully booked trans-Atlantic ocean liners. As he deals in magnificent art with crass American *arrivistes,* however, Pengo himself is in a race with death. In the emotionally tense final scene, he swallows a tablet that will presumably forestall his demise; he then makes a grand departure from his gallery-studio, leaving Miss Swanson and a few art objects in his wake.

An audience is bound to view Pengo with a certain ambivalence. His strong belief in himself and in his ability to negotiate sales at an enormous profit reveals that, in one sense, he is no ordinary man. His son Derek also realizes this fact, and he knows that he will never quite equal his father. Reminiscent of Philip Talley in *The Talley*

Method, Derek admits to his father in the first act that "it's like a great physician who leaves his practice to a son who hasn't got the bedside manner." Pengo, in reality, is scarcely superior to his vulgar customers who, like himself, are but glorified hucksters; Pengo has at least two characteristics that his customers lack—a superficial flair and polish.

According to Maurice Zolotow, Behrman's last play, *But for Whom Charlie*, was "conceived . . . with Lynn and Alfred [Lunt] in mind."[33] The play opened without them, however, at the Repertory Theater at Lincoln Center on March 12, 1964. Richard Watts, Jr., perhaps recalling *Lord Pengo*, recognized that the chief problem in Behrman's newest and last play was "the conflict between opportunism and integrity."[34] Behrman's subject was life in one of the large philanthropic New York foundations organized to render financial encouragement to worthy scholars and artists. The scene is the East Sixties at the Seymour Rosenthal Foundation where characters assemble for verbal excursions that take all of the familiar Behrman directions. Marriage, of course, is among the central issues, although there is much more talk of marriage than there is marriage itself. There are also two cases of conflict between father and son.

The play concerns young, promiscuous Faith Prosper, who comes to Charles Taney, director of the Rosenthal Foundation, about securing a grant for her alcoholic brother, the scholar Willard Prosper. Willard, it turns out, has lived too long in the shadow of his late father's artistic career. In the final act, Behrman reveals that Willard as a child had vowed to kill his father, and that Seymour Rosenthal himself is haunted by the memory of his own father. Taney explains to Gillian Prosper, step-mother to Faith and Willard, that Seymour's father had been an "overwhelming, monstrous Napoleonic" person "of whom he [Seymour] was ashamed."

Behrman's last play partly involves the character of Brock Dunaway, who is introduced in the second act as "a spry seventy, little, nimble, with a sharp, glittering eye." Dunaway is evidently another self-portrait: a wry, witty, Jewish gentleman and novelist, he reminisces about his early days in Hollywood and refers to himself as "an extinct volcano." The relationship between Faith Prosper and her step-mother Gillian is still another instance of the juxtaposing of youth and maturity that had been apparent in such plays as *The Second Man*, *The Talley Method*, and *Jane*. Gillian herself is another, and the last, of Behrman's emancipated women.

But for Whom Charlie contains, uncharacteristically for Behrman, a quantity of frankly sexual dialogue, which may perhaps be attributed more to theatrical tastes of the 1960s than to the playwright. In one of the opening speeches, for example, Charles Taney complains in a telephone conversation about his "post-coitum melancholia." In act III, Gillian admits to having met her ex-husband after he had seen her posing in the nude in a pornographic film. Not since *Amphitryon 38*, obviously a very different kind of play, had emphasis upon the sexual been so pronounced.

As had been true in so many of the plays after 1936, *But for Whom Charlie* manages not to lead anywhere. The play is probably best summed up in John McCarten's review for *The New Yorker* in which he calls it "a rather shapeless seriocomic work in which modern opportunism is pitted against sound, old fashioned honesty."[35] With a run of forty-seven performances, *But for Whom Charlie* joined *Wine of Choice* and *Dunnigan's Daughter* as the three least well received plays in the Behrman canon.

CHAPTER 5

Maturity and Reflection:
The Prose Pieces

"I have one hobby: it is writing prose," Behrman told a reporter for the *New York Herald Tribune Book Review* in 1954. "Playwriting," he continued, "is the most difficult form of writing for a living there is. It is governed by an inexorable geometry and, if you violate the essentials of that geometry nothing will save you: neither wit, nor grace, nor imagination, nor style."[1] Behrman's stronger and artistically better literary genre, ironically enough, was the prose essay, and but few Americans—E. B. White, James Thurber, H. L. Mencken, S. J. Perelman—can rival Behrman in his handling of this fading literary form. In his essays, not in his dramas, Behrman was able, in a sense, to come to terms with himself, to say what he felt most deeply, and to comprehend the meaning of his own life.

The early prose pieces are most often biographical, but the essayist himself is revealed only by the character of his language and by the intelligence of his perceptions. All told, his prose essays move almost uninterruptedly from anonymity to self-realization; but this progression is not found in the plays. The prose pieces range from occasional essays written about external subjects (while an undergraduate at Clark) to the keenly introspective memoirs.

Behrman's prose, including his one novel, is contained in six volumes. *The Suspended Drawing Room,* while not collected and issued until 1965, contains the earliest of his better essays. With the exception of two pieces on Gabriel Pascal and Bernard Shaw, *The Suspended Drawing Room* essays were written between 1939 and 1947; and of the twelve pieces included, nine had appeared originally in *The New Yorker. The Worcester Account,* which consists of eleven autobiographical installments published in *The New Yorker* during an eight-year period following the end of World War II, was issued in 1954. In 1951, Behrman's six-part series for *The New*

Yorker entitled "The Days of Duveen" was published by Random House as *Duveen*. Then in February and March, 1960, his seven essays on Max Beerbohm for *The New Yorker* appeared under the general title of *Portrait of Max*, published also by Random House. In 1960, came his none-too-successful autobiographical novel called *The Burning Glass*; it was followed by his memoirs, *People in a Diary*, that was published in three issues of *The New Yorker* in May, 1972.

Because the essays eventually included in *The Suspended Drawing Room*, *The Worchester Account*, and *Duveen* overlap in the time in which they were written, it is difficult to generalize about the growth and development of Behrman's prose style. There are, nevertheless, some other observations that should be made besides those in chapter 7 of this study. It is possible, as has been mentioned, to see the gradual emergence of Behrman the person in his own writing. In his early prose, in which he had remained well in the background, he plays the part of the unobtrusive observer who gives his attention mostly to biographical subjects. In *The Suspended Drawing Room*, he is more than a reporter, but he is scarcely an active participant in what he sees. In *Portrait of Max*, Behrman engages in conversations with Max Beerbohm that reveal only a little less about himself than they do about his friend. *The Burning Glass*, of course, places Behrman in center stage, although he represents himself as a fictional character. Behrman reveals himself most fully in the memoirs, *People in a Diary*.

I   The Suspended Drawing Room

The apprenticeship pieces treated in chapter 2 contain the general characteristics of his later prose essays. Behrman always attached much importance to success, especially to that achieved through the fortunate convergence of superior ability and uncommon dedication. This emphasis partly explains why seven of *The Suspended Drawing Room* essays concern men who have risen in the world from ostensibly humble beginnings. The two pieces about Gabriel Pascal dwell upon his skill in manipulating and persuading George Bernard Shaw to allow him the film rights to his plays; one essay centers on the inspiring personality of the Zionist Chaim Weizman; and the extraordinary New York physician Dr. Emanuel Libman is the subject of another portrait, one that verges upon the idolatrous. Other admiring essays concentrate upon Robert Sher-

wood, A. E. Kazan, and Ferenc Molnar, all of whom Behrman treats
with admiration, if not adulation.

The subjects of Behrman's biographical essays, of course, possess
characteristics other than achievement of success. All are men, and
none of them can be considered young. Many of the subjects of the
portraits—Pascal, Weizman, Libman, and Molnar, for example—
are not wholly assimilated into the American scene, and all are
eccentric in certain respects. Behrman, for example, evinces a particular interest in Dr. Libman's unusual dining habits: "He thinks
that certain restaurants are best for certain dishes and he will sometimes have soup or hors d'oeuvres in one, go to another for the roast,
and still another for dessert and coffee. He is fond of boiled potatoes
and will go to a restaurant because it serves good boiled potatoes. Or
he will have a run on black pepper and will go places that are using it
in their cooking."

The most accurate and appropriate word to describe the essays is
"civilized," and the quality that makes them so is the author's earnest concern for people, especially those who are—like George
Gershwin, Eddie Cantor, and Harold Ross—spirited, colorful, enthusiastic. The element of success that Behrman applauds is not
necessarily to be measured in economic terms; for, as in *The Worcester Account*, a number of his sketches are devoted to otherwise
unknown people who are notably successful at being alive. But, with
his subject characters, he prefers to concentrate upon what is frequently the humorous anecdote, a method which enlivens his por-
traiture. Of his friend Robert Sherwood, for example, he wrote with
a certain gentle humor in *The Suspended Drawing Room:*

As an infant, Sherwood seems to have been a chore. He was secretive and
shy, and he had a mind and a code of his own. Once he was discovered in a
room in which his bedridden grandmother was ensconced in a wheelchair.
The child was manipulating a fishing pole, to the end of which was attached
a piece of string neatly tied around a live beetle. With this beetle he was
gently caressing grandmother's face at long range. She was doing her best to
dodge and was calling out feebly from time to time, half in laughter and half
in fear. To a horrified inquiry about what he was doing, he replied calmly,
"I'm tickling up Grandma."

Behrman recommends the virtue of tolerance as much in the
essays as in the plays, and he does so to the extent that tolerance
becomes part of his point of view. Where his biographical subjects

are concerned, he makes no effort either to whitewash or to conceal, but he is not prone to censure or criticize in a serious way. He may say, for instance, that Gabriel Pascal was sometimes rude to waiters, or that Robert Sherwood was considered by some to be a bore; but his criticism scarcely ever becomes more adverse than that.

Two parts of the book ("The Suspended Drawing Room" and "It's Cold at Lady Windermere's") are devoted to considerations of "time and place," for the subject turns to London during the Blitz. Behrman's generally tolerant and sympathetic attitude toward people applies to the whole wartime population of London. The unfailing courage and the indomitable spirit of the British during the Nazi air attacks easily captured Behrman's admiration. His anecdote about the opening night of Somerset Maugham's *The Circle* and the air-raid alert tells a good deal about the fabled character of the English population under the emotional stress of a bombing raid:

> The sirens began. In front of the footlights a square transparency lit up to reveal the word "ALERT" in huge block letters—quite unnecessarily, it seemed to me, as the sirens were distinctly audible. Lady Kitty had been describing the shabbier social aspects of life in Monte Carlo. I half expected Yvonne Arnaud, playing Lady Kitty, to say, "My dear Elizabeth, go to the nearest shelter at once." But Lady Kitty didn't. She went on frequently imploring Elizabeth to avoid scandal. No one in the audience stirred, except to strain forward a bit to hear Yvonne Arnaud better.

The characters, the speech patterns, and the settings of Behrman plays in the 1930s, especially in *Serena Blandish* and in *Rain from Heaven*, indicate the playwright's attraction to the cultured, civilized aspects of English life. These plays, along with *Jane*, had used English manners to some comic advantage; but Behrman's interest in England is also an expression of his cosmopolitan spirit that easily transcends a narrow identification with America. Significantly, the essay entitled "It's Cold at Lady Windermere's" includes a remark about England's "young and rebellious Parliamentarians" that seems to capture the essence of what Behrman admired about the English: "They see an England that, almost alone in the world between the converging colossi of Russian Communism and American Capitalism, will keep alive the free, inquiring, individual, humanistic spirit. . . . They see, without being in the least pompous about it, an England emerging from a series of temporary crises, an

England that will never succumb to a totalitarianism of either the Right or the Left and that will perpetuate its best traditions." Obviously enough, similarity exists between the political message in the plays, especially of the 1930s and 1940s, and what is plainly stated here. Behrman's moderate stance between extreme political polarization is a position he never altered.

II   The Worcester Account

With the single exception of chapter II ("Providence Street in Summer"), *The Worcester Account* (1954) is the combined product of a series of related essays from *The New Yorker* that were printed between June 29, 1946, and June 5, 1954. That the essays were arranged in the book in an order different from their original sequence indicates that *The Worcester Account* was something of an afterthought. But, aside from one or two minor inconsistencies and repetitions, there is little to suggest that the book suffers from either stylistic or structural disunity. The unity of the volume is achieved through the author's focusing attention upon the richly individualistic human beings he had known as a child in Worcester, especially his father, Willie Lavin, and Dr. Nightingale, the family physician. The entire milieu—the people, the times, the circumstances, the environment—are subjected, however, to some slight alteration requisite to the transformation of raw experience into finished aesthetic form.

While *The Worcester Account* dwells upon a good many dilemmas and predicaments among the denizens of old Providence Street, the reader is exposed perhaps above all to the religious orthodoxy of Behrman's childhood and to the inevitable conflict between it and the Protestant Ethic which surrounds the area. Behrman treats his experiences in the Worcester public schools and then moves on to Clark, Harvard, and Columbia. He mentions something of the books he read, the places he frequented, and the people who influenced him the most.

Above all, *The Worcester Account* is a book for reading. The warmth and charm of it are often to be found in the manner in which the sometimes loosely related parts are narrated. The book is a pleasantly compassionate statement that expresses more about Behrman's early years than do any other specimens of his finished prose works. Here, perhaps more than in any other place, he expresses his intensely human, deep concern for those who shared the experience of minority life in an American industrial city around the turn of the century. The singular beauty of the book is its language. His prose style is at its best in the second chapter where Behrman discusses the streets that lead in various directions from his own:

Our street, Providence, led to all these streets. And these led to country roads and these country roads led to other streets. And these streets were in other cities which lay beyond one's reach, but capturable through some not impossible twist in the veiled future. Palmer and Springfield, Ware and Woonsocket, Northampton and Framingham—what manner of places were these? There were no motor cars then and the roads that led to these far cities could not be burned up; they had to be travelled, they had to be traversed. We knew we would come to them in time, these strange places; they would be conquered in time; they beckoned from the haze and shimmer of the horizon.

The Worcester Account confirms the message implicit in the plays—that his central concern is people, often the more eccentric and enigmatic individuals who are seen at their best. Unlike some of the profiles done for *The New Yorker* (e.g., Beerbohm and Duveen), these passing memory portraits of men and women do not concentrate upon the wealthy and famous but upon the otherwise unheralded personalities who in the dim past occupied the Jewish district of Worcester. Perhaps in his full maturity as a writer, Behrman had reached the point where he could write with intense conviction about people other than the famous and the wealthy. Indeed, Behrman lets it be known in *The Worcester Account* that the meaningful life is the one lived with verve and commitment; and those who inhabit its world are vivid, passionate, strenuous souls, intense in their approach to everyday life.

Behrman could now write, of course, with the security of knowing that he had safely broken free of the social and economic limitations imposed by Providence Street. One of the characteristics of his apprenticeship writing had been the frequently expressed fear of not being able to escape the dreary life that the New England industrial city seemed to promise. His early fiction had been written from the point of view of a young writer unsure of his talent and destiny. But even from the vantage point of security and fame, Behrman was not yet willing to fully reveal himself or his background.

III   Duveen

In 1944, William Shawn, one of *The New Yorker* editors, suggested to Behrman that he write a book about Joseph Duveen, the international art dealer who had died in 1939. Duveen was a natural subject for Behrman; the portraits in *The Suspended Drawing Room* showed that his taste in people gravitated toward those who were foreign-born, unusually "successful," and, most of all, irrepressible in character. Seen in the light of these early portraits, Behrman's interest in the life and style of Joseph Duveen becomes more understandable.

Not much unlike *Portrait of Max* in its objectives, *Duveen* is no ordinary, systematic, chronological biography; Behrman provides an account of Duveen's initiation as an art dealer and the circumstances that converged to make him the preeminent purveyor of art treasures in his time to the newly rich American millionaires. Duveen himself remains squarely in the center of the book, however, and his story is fundamentally another treatment of the myth of humble beginnings that had interested Behrman since his youth, when he had pored over the Horatio Alger stories. Moreover, Duveen's heritage, like that of his biographer, reached far back into European Jewry.

Besides being in some respects an object lesson in how to rise in the world, the Duveen story contains other elements common in Behrman's writing. Money and wealth hold a prominent place in the book, and there is still wonderment in the biographer's tone as he intermingles high culture and big money. Duveen is another of Behrman's matrimonially unattached individuals who bargains for high stakes in international circles without the restriction and encumbrance of a wife. Along with Gabriel Pascal, Duveen possesses the extraordinary ability to manipulate people to his own advantage. While Duveen may have been at heart what Behrman called "a lovable buccaneer," Duveen is nevertheless credited with having played a role in the civilizing of America. Behrman notes in his first chapter that Duveen "forced American collectors to accumulate great things, infused them with a fierce pride in collecting, and finally got their collections into museums, making it possible for the American people to see a large share of the world's most beautiful art without having to go abroad."

Behrman also emphasizes that, temperamentally, Duveen and his customers were worlds apart. At the beginning of the book Behrman lets it be known that "the great American millionaires of the Duveen Era were slow-speaking and slow-thinking, cautious, secretive—in Duveen's eyes maddeningly deliberate. . . . For a man like Duveen, who was congenitally unable to keep quiet, the necessity of dealing constantly with cryptic men like the elder J. P. Morgan and Henry Clay Frick and [Andrew] Mellon was ulcerating." But, although Duveen found it difficult at times to tolerate his philistine customers, it becomes evident that the book is also a double-edged portrait containing, along with its human-interest elements, a goodly measure of implicit and explicit criticism of the American preoccupation with wealth. In the very first paragraph Behrman provides in theory the simple formula for Duveen's immense, uncanny talent for marketing art objects. Duveen had observed, Behrman says, "that Europe had plenty of art and America had plenty of money." In the final pages, his point is made even clearer: "a lovable buccaneer" like Duveen could only have done so well under the prosperous, but often unhappy, circumstances made possible by American industrialism:

The millionaires of the Duveen Era were all dressed up, but they really had no place to go. Duveen supplied a favored few of them with a destination. The private lives of the sad tycoons were often bitter; their children and their family life disappointed them. The fathers had too much to give; the returns were often in reverse ratio to the size of the gifts. They knew that they were ruining their children and yet they didn't know how to stop it. Their children made disastrous marriages, got killed in racing cars, had to pay blackmail to avoid scandal. But with the works of art it was different. They asked for nothing. They were rewarding. They shed their radiance, and it was a lovely, soothing sight. . . .

As Behrman notes in his third chapter, "Duveen outmonopolized the monopolists who were among his biggest clients." Among those monopolists with whom he had dealings was Henry Ford, who is described in *Duveen* in chapter 6 ("The Silent Men") as preferring an advertising brochure of one hundred reproduced paintings to the original paintings themselves. In short, the vulgarized materialism and the distorted value system inherent in American life are placed in contrast to the urbane (but perhaps not fully authentic) cosmopolitan image fostered by Duveen himself. Mindful of this contrast, it is useful to consider *The New Yorker* audience for whom

"The Days of Duveen" series was originally written. Like the personalities who once surrounded Duveen himself, readers of *The New Yorker* were more often than not composed of members of the upper economic class. The frequent but often subtle questioning by writers for *The New Yorker* of American values was undoubtedly aimed as much at the general readership as it was at men like Henry Ford, J. P. Morgan, C. P. Huntington, and their ilk.

In placing *Duveen* within the context of Behrman's other work, it is not difficult to see that Behrman had once more found a man who, by intelligence, diligence, and sheer nerve, had become a figure as representative of authority and prestige as most of the other portraits that Behrman had written for *The New Yorker*. Behrman's enthusiasm for his biographical subject this time was motivated less by admiration than by fascination. All considered, *Duveen* is a civilized and intelligent book written to be appreciated by a limited audience.

IV   Portrait of Max

Book reviewers took kindly to *Duveen;* and Max Beerbohm who read the book with some interest in Rapallo, Italy, wrote Behrman an appreciative letter. Behrman, who responded by sending Beerbohm an autographed copy of the work, was greeted in turn by an invitation from Beerbohm to visit Rapallo, which he did in 1952, 1953, 1954, and 1955. "I don't remember," Beerbohm said of Behrman, "having met in my later years anybody who appealed to me as this charming magnetic man has."[2] The feeling was mutual. Behrman saw in his aging friend the irresistible attributes of wit, keen intelligence, discriminating good taste, honest individuality, warmth, graciousness, and abundant character. He was, in short, Behrman's ideal of the fully civilized man whose view of the world coincided with Behrman's own high regard for the humane, the tolerant, and the comic.

Along with the very funny Beerbohm caricatures in *Portrait of Max*, a few well-chosen specimens of his prose style reveal a special affinity to Behrman's own rhetoric. It gradually becomes apparent not only that the two men envisioned the world in the same terms but that they also wrote much alike. Both styles capture a certain nineteenth-century flavor, both evince a cosmopolitan character, and both concentrate upon the subtle and comic anecdote. Behrman's handling of dialogue, it hardly need be said, owes a great deal to his dramatic writing. At one point in the book, for example, the subject is Behrman's proposal that Max's works should be reissued in a new edition:

. . . I had discussed with a friend the possibility of getting all of Max's works together in a Modern Library Giant. I now told Max about this project. I explained to him that there were Giant Faulkners, Giant Hemingways, and so on.

"How would you like to be a Giant, Sir Max?" I asked.

"I should have to get an entirely new wardrobe," he said regretfully, with an air of a man who already has all the clothes he wants.

In the sixth chapter ("The Executive Forefinger"), Behrman turns to portrait painting and to John Singer Sargent; and Max recalls an appropriate anecdote: "But Sargent! One night, at some dinner, he was asked about portrait painting. He began to heave and pant, but he did not get out an amusing definition. 'Oh—Portraits—A portrait painting—' Max finally gasped it out: 'A portrait is a painting where there's always something not quite right about the mouth'."

Both *Duveen* and *Portrait of Max* consist primarily of isolated scenes and spirited exchanges of witty dialogue. In *Portrait of Max*, Behrman has composed a series of loosely related personality sketches that tend to delineate Beerbohm's engaging manner. The book ends with an account of Max's death and with the surprising disclosure of his secret marriage to Miss Jungman, his benevolent secretary-companion. Behrman's final paragraph is particularly effective. Earlier, he had mentioned Beerbohm's caricature of Arnold Bennett as an "old self" addressing Arnold Bennett as a "young self," and, with that sketch in mind, Behrman renders Max himself as old and young self. Of the day of Max's death, Behrman writes, that "the Old Self could safely have taken off the mask of the character that the Young Self had created—the character of Max Beerbohm. The discrepancy between the man and the mask was always slighter in Max than in most people, and by that time the two had become indistinguishable. Under the Maxian mask was, ultimately, Max."

V The Burning Glass

A veiled announcement of Behrman's intention to write an autobiographical novel appears in his final play *But for Whom Charlie*

in 1964. At the opening of the second act, Seymour Rosenthal of the
Rosenthal Foundation discusses the chances of Brock Dunaway's
arranging a renewal of his writing grant. "He must be well over
seventy," Rosenthal argues; "and he's working on a book which will
summarize, he says, all his experience of life. It's considerable—that
experience." When Behrman's career as dramatic writer ended, he
sought somehow to capture the flavor of his life and time in a single
artistic effort. *The Cold Wind and the Warm,* although it was
impressionistically autobiographical, had by no means communi-
cated all that Behrman felt about himself and his relationship with
the world. Evidently the limitations of the stage forced him to seek a
broader and less restricted literary genre that would permit the use
over a period of years of a still larger number of characters in different geographical locations. The only appropriate vehicle was the
novel, even though Behrman (now past his seventieth birthday) had
never before attempted to write one. "But it is," he mistakenly
insisted later, ". . . much more difficult to write a good play than it is
to write a good novel."[3] *The Burning Glass* (1968), published during
Behrman's seventy-fifth year, was also the result of his long-
contemplated desire to write a novel.

The significance of the title seems to come from the second chapter of *Portrait of Max,* in which Behrman recounts an incident
wherein he and Max are standing before a mirror which "infoliated
the images and focused them, as in a burning glass." The book is,
then, an attempt to synthesize somehow his "experience of life" into
a coherent, unified artistic form. Behrman selected the critical
three-year period extending from the Salzburg Festival of 1937 to
the outbreak of World War II, and the setting is especially significant. Part I of the novel treats the protagonist Stanley Grant's
sojourn in Austria where "the Jewish question" hung ominously in
the air and where uniformed Nazis were omnipresent in the concert
hall, in the restaurants, in the shops. In part II, set in New York and
Hollywood, Behrman populates his novel with the colorful but
erratic personalities connected with the motion-picture colony of
the 1930s. As in the plays, he provides once again a cosmopolitan
cast of characters, most of them economically and socially privileged.

The novel is paved with good intentions; and, while not an artistic
success, it tells a great deal about Behrman and his career. The
theme of the book is Stanley Grant's affirmation of his Jewishness.
Grant himself is a young and newly successful American playwright,

obviously another Behrman self-portrait. Like Behrman, he has managed to rise from humble origins, but he does not come from industrial New England but from the Middle West—from Xenia, Ohio. The name "Stanley Grant," it later becomes known, is a pseudonym calculated to conceal his Jewish identity; and the thrust of the novel is directed at Grant's inner turmoil over his Jewishness and his general understanding of himself. He finally reaffirms his racial identity by acknowledging and proudly embracing his authentic name: Jacob Ben Sion Trynin. In the final page of the novel, he bids a "farewell to the shades of Sir Henry Morton Stanley and Ulysses S. Grant" from whose names he had fabricated his own. "Perhaps now," the reader is told, "he might find out who he was."

Behrman makes much of Grant's provincial background, referring to him in the opening chapter as "a recent nonentity from Xenia, Ohio." Unlikely though it is that a Jewish immigrant family would choose to settle in a midwestern town, Behrman selected Xenia as an example of provincial America. Stanley Grant's preference, like Behrman's, is for a higher level of sophistication, and part of Grant's object in visiting Salzburg, after all, is the prospect of his staying with the millionairess Stephanie von Arnim at her country estate.

The Burning Glass abounds in autobiographical elements. The Behrmans had also attended the Salzburg Festival on the eve of World War II, as has been mentioned; and in Austria their son David Arthur was born. Stanley Grant's child is also delivered in an Austrian hospital, but in the novel the child is born out of wedlock. Like Behrman, Grant is especially conscious of his past; and he hopes never again to experience the "squalid tenement" conditions in which he had matured. Neither has Grant forgotten "the poverty, nor the ghetto grayness, nor the self doubt." He worries habitually, as Behrman apparently had, about his future. He broods also about his self-image: "awkward, odd-looking, unattractive." He suffers from "a mild recurrent acne" condition. In spite of his Harvard degree, he feels himself "uneducated." The lack of physical coordination also causes him to feel foolish; and, like Behrman himself, Grant "fainted easily from the time he was in high school." He has a decidedly ambivalent feeling toward science and scientists; but, at the same time, he regrets his "shallow" literary studies in college. Like Behrman in the 1930s, Grant becomes "probably the only writer in Hollywood who had a sneaking sympathy for his bosses, the tycoons."

As might be expected, Behrman's long-held attitudes and opinions appear in the novel virtually unaltered from what they had been in his earlier writing. Money plays a large role in the book, and "have-not" Stanley Grant is duly impressed with what money can do for him; but he recognizes, eventually, that money will not solve all his problems. Even so, as his friend and advisor Alexander Löwe alleges with a note of irony in the first chapter, "there are very few calamities in life in which the possession of money is not a considerable mitigation." Grant, like a number of other Behrman characters, evades marriage. If it had not been for Löwe's insistence that he do the proper thing, Grant's eventual marriage to Eileen, the mother of his son, might never have occurred; for Grant fears that marriage will threaten his artistic ambitions. In chapter 10, Grant "wanted to go back to the United States right away. But then he couldn't. He had a baby in the hospital, and a bride. He was trapped."

A reader at all familiar with Behrman's canon of plays recognizes immediately that *The Burning Glass* is replete with fragments of the plays from over the years. From *The Second Man,* for example, Behrman uses the aspiring young (temporarily unattached) writer caught between eligible matrimonial prospects but who, at the same time, fears marriage. From *Meteor,* there is the protagonist who conceals his real identity by altering his name. In the thirteenth chapter of *The Burning Glass,* there is a reference to the character Rutherford Lord who is in some respects like Raphael Lord in *Meteor.* As in *Biography* and other plays, the reader is habitually aware of the threat posed by rampant fascism. Thaddeus Willens, referred to in the twenty-third chapter, calls to mind another "citoyen du monde," Hugo Willens in *Rain from Heaven.*

There are also a number of echoes from *Rain from Heaven;* for example, the "oil-millionaires from Cleveland" are reminiscent of old Mrs. Wyler. Dr. Kenneth Ogden in *The Burning Glass* seems to be another version of Dr. Kenneth Rice in *End of Summer.* In the fourth chapter, Behrman has Stanley Grant preparing to write a play which will be set "in the midst of the depression," and he contemplates placing his characters in a house located on the "masculine Riviera" of Maine. In chapter 31, some actual lines are cited from Grant's new play which, though not named, is *End of Summer.* Behrman's remark in the second chapter that Eileen believes "she is having an affair with Zeus" recalls the physical union of mortal and immortal in *Amphitryon 38.*

Behrman's reference to "mechanical hearts" (chapter 23) is the original title of *The Talley Method*. Grant's recollection of his father, "a simple, ineffectual, pure man, secure in the embrace of the Almighty" (chapter 4) must surely come from the pages of *The Worcester Account*, as does Grant's fear of the dreaded "Malach H'Amovis, the Angel of Death" in the fourth chapter of *The Burning Glass*. Certain of *The New Yorker* "profiles" also find their way into the novel. Chaim Weizman, for example, is mentioned by name in chapter 4; and Dr. Leo Binder, Dr. Emanuel Libman, and Robert Sherwood figure elsewhere in the novel.

Unfortunately, *The Burning Glass* elicited something less than enthusiastic reaction from reviewers, and the general reaction was that the novel suffered from the same flaws that had detracted from the plays. Some found the novel too diffuse; it had too many characters who contributed too little. Ruth Gambee considered *The Burning Glass* to be "tedious, confused and carelessly written."[4] Granville Hicks surmised that Behrman must have felt "that his experiences had been rich enough to make an interesting novel, and to that extent he was right." He continued, however, by saying that "I suppose he told himself [that] novelists can get away with murder."[5]

However, the reviews in *Time* and *The New Yorker* were less severe. The anonymously written *Time* review called the novel's ending "an embarrassing cliché," but the reviewer also added that Behrman's "mastery of dialogue shines on every page."[6] Naomi Bliven of *The New Yorker* somewhat ironically claimed that Behrman had brought "two gifts that a playwright can bring to fiction—structure and concision."[7] The pity was that what appeared at this point to be the capstone of Behrman's career was not all that it might have been. In retrospect, it seemed to Behrman not to have been a good idea in the first place. "I am always lost in admiration of people who can do things that I can't do," Behrman wrote later, "like solving mathematical problems or writing novels."[8]

VI People in a Diary

If certain prose essays constitute the best of S. N. Behrman's work, then the memoirs, entitled *People in a Diary* (1972), are the best of his prose works. The progression and the continuity of the memoirs in their relationship to the content, tone, and style of Behrman's earlier prose essays is clear enough. Always conversational, anecdotal, pointed, and ingeniously selective, the essays that combine to form Behrman's memoirs resonate between the richly funny and the profoundly sad.

The raw materials for *People in a Diary* were the sixty-odd volumes of his personal diary which Behrman had maintained faithfully since 1915, during his Harvard days, but the memoirs themselves are the product of intermittent work in the decade between his seventieth and eightieth birthdays. Like the earlier essays, these are concerned exclusively with people; however, Behrman is more inclined to view them in their relationship to himself than ever before; and he considers the various influences of different individuals in the shaping of his own destiny. In the earlier "profiles" he had tended to look at people as private identities and to keep his role as commentator somewhat guarded and usually well in the background. The memoirs, moreover, are the final step in Behrman's tendency to focus attention upon himself rather than upon others.

"An odd quirk of destiny has put a great many people in my way," he comments at the conclusion of his initial essay. "I want, in this book, to return to them. I want to revive their society, to share their tribulations and their laughter." After this remark, a remarkable and varied cavalcade of personalities passes before the reader; and among them are Siegfried Sassoon, Jed Harris, Marc Connelly, the Lunts, director Philip Moeller, George and Ira Gershwin, Jean Giraudoux, Arnold Bennett, Alexander Woollcott, Ina Claire, Greta Garbo, Laurence Olivier, Katherine Cornell, Louis B. Mayer, Franz Werfel, Noel Coward, Robert Sherwood, Maxwell Anderson, Sidney Howard, Elmer Rice, Eugene O'Neill, Harold Ross, Felix Frankfurter, Groucho and Harpo Marx, Bernard Berenson, Somerset Maugham, Harold Laski, John F. Kennedy, and others of comparable achievement.

Behrman manages in the memoirs to steer around most of the people and the anecdotes he had stressed in *Duveen, The Worcester Account, Portrait of Max, The Suspended Drawing Room,* and *The Burning Glass.* His childhood friend Daniel Asher is not even mentioned, and there are other curious omissions: Behrman disposes of his marriage to Elza Heifetz in a single sentence in the seventeenth chapter: "I had married Elza, the younger Heifetz girl." He mentions his son not at all, and his brothers but once.

Except in *The Burning Glass,* Behrman was never one to be

bound to a strictly chronological progression of events. In the memoirs, he moves gracefully back and forward in time, relating and comparing faces and circumstances with the ease of one who is more concerned with significances than with dates. The result is a somewhat murky sense of time in the essays; indeed, few specific years are cited in his recollections. "Every playwright is hemmed in, in space and time, by the first words he has to write at the beginning of every play: AT RISE, SCENE, TIME," he comments at the opening of the final chapter. One's life, he says, is better understood by cycles than by the uninterrupted turning of the years: "the rises and falls within our lives, the innumerable re-births and renewals, from the mock deaths of depression to the plateaus of self-belief, the diminuendos and crescendos of the psyche."

Tonally, the memoirs combine a certain sweetness of remem-brance with a dash of irony. Then at the age of eighty, Behrman admits at the beginning of the book that "I have had just about all I can take of myself. I am a mild manic-depressive, difficult at times to distinguish from an acute one." In the twenty-second chapter, he conveys his thoughts during a period of painful hospital convales-cence late in his life: "Among the chronic self-reproaches that re-turned to plague me during those merciless nights, which I thought would be my last, was that I had spent too much time in Hollywood. . . I felt that I had wasted my life. . . ."

The purpose of *People in a Diary*, like that of all memoirs, is to leave a part of one's essence and experience behind and to offer some remarks about the condition of man in the inscrutable uni-verse he inhabits. Of people, Behrman concludes in chapter 12, "I have known very busy ones, rich ones, triumphant ones, but few who have been contented." Of America, he wrote with reference to her involvement in Southeast Asia, "the country has taken on a frightening aspect. It seems to have become a plutocracy, cruel, capable of atrocities, which has darkened its image all over the world." Consistent with everything that he had ever written, how-ever, the memoirs are intended to please and to inform intelligent-ly, with grace and wit, with candor and compassion.

CHAPTER 6

The Major Themes

THE plays and the prose essays of S. N. Behrman lend themselves rather neatly and conveniently to a study of thematic continuity. After the reader has familiarized himself with Behrman's set of values and priorities as expressed in his various publications, he realizes that the playwright's entire output of literature tends to fall into specific categories. Moreover, as is sometimes true with other men of letters, his prevailing vision of the world was modified very little between the middle 1920s and 1972 when his last book appeared, although gradual thematic shifts occurred during these years.

I *Ascendancy*

As has been noted frequently, Behrman's basic life experience is mirrored in his writing. Chapter 1 explained that he was the youngest of three sons of immigrant Eastern European Jewish parents who came to America in the 1890s. Given the circumstances of his heritage and his life in Worcester, Massachusetts, it is not surprising that the Joseph Behrman family would have been motivated to "make good" in their newly adopted environment. Although Joseph himself enjoyed very limited economic success, his two older sons were destined to thrive in their accounting firm. Indications are that S. N. Behrman, as a young man, was painfully aware, at least until 1927, of his apparent failure to show much promise as a young writer; but certain self-doubt remained with him always. In his memoirs he wrote that

I have been haunted by dreams of poverty all my life, through all the years since I emerged from it. I dream that I am in hotel rooms without the money to pay for them. I dream that I am jobless and can't get a job. A favorite disagreeable dream is that I am walking in a heavy rain, and carrying a leaden suitcase, from Boston to Worcester. When I get to Worcester there is nowhere to go. Everyone is dead. I go to the Bancroft Hotel, go up in the elevator, and walk down a corridor. Exhausted from the walk, my shoes and my clothes soaking, I open a door, see a bed, and sink down on it. Then I see that the room contains somebody else's possessions. I must not fall asleep, lest the occupant come in. I struggle to remain awake. I fall asleep. . . .

Elsewhere in the memoirs Behrman admitted, "I never shook off the plaintive counterpoint of my origins—the memory of my parents, and their poverty."

That problems concerning ascendancy in the world appear frequently in his writing is therefore quite understandable. His first writing efforts had not infrequently dealt with the problems and frustrations of getting ahead in America. Later, in *The Second Man,* the future of Clark Storey's artistic career is an unusually sensitive subject with him. *Meteor* almost single-mindedly treats the problems and moral sacrifices necessary to get to the top in the capitalistic system, and *Serena Blandish* contains some damnably ruthless guidelines for the success-oriented individual. Here, of course, the specific problem concerns the compromises necessary to place a poor girl in the upper reaches of the London social and economic scene. Like *Serena Blandish, Brief Moment* also bears heavily on the more subtle ramifications of the success myth. Roderick Dean, the ineffective rich boy of the play, laments in the first act that he is "surrounded by successful people" with whom he can ill compete. In *Biography,* the words "success" and "successful" appear frequently. Bunny Nolan assures Marion Froude in the first act, for example, that "I've been pretty successful in the law. Tremendously successful, I may say."

Both *Rain from Heaven* and *End of Summer* dwell at length on the unexpected results of what appears to be success. In the first play, Hugo Willens has written a book about a little-known playwright and has brought more "success" to himself than to the playwright. Will Dexter says in the first act of *End of Summer* that he has been elected "as the one most likely to succeed" by his classmates, a doubly ironic remark in view of the play's Depression background. Will's father, in still another ironic remark, declares that he has been fired for having been too successful at chipping "off a fragment of knowledge, a truth which so-called practical men may put to . . . use." Similarly, *The Talley Method* deals with the ironic rewards of being "rich and successful": Dr. Talley's preeminence in medicine serves only to alienate him from all but his most devoted patients.

Not in the least ironic, however, is Wilda Doran's line in the final act of *Wine of Choice* when she, addressing Dow Christophsen, assures him that "I had to make my way out of poverty—just as you did—I came out of nothing—just as you did—I had to stand indescribable—I can stand it again." The subject of success is also very much on the mind of Linda Esterbrook as she speaks to Amanda Smith in *No Time for Comedy:* "Why," she inquires, "do you always pick arrivés to inspire? Your husband was rich and successful when you married him. My husband is an established writer, temporarily in the dumps. Why don't you stimulate to greatness someone obscure?"

Throughout Behrman's plays, the basic questing after success is approached from two sides. The first is through the point of view of those who have only recently captured what in *Wine of Choice* he calls "the heavy odor of success." The other point of view derives from having lived with success for so long that it has become the usual thing. *Meteor* and *Dunnigan's Daughter* both show that, when success is quickly and unscrupulously gained, it can contain the seeds of its own destruction. But, as the portraits in *The Suspended Drawing Room* suggest, permanent and genuine success falls to those on whom it rests well: persons with talent and industry to offer in return for it. It becomes apparent in *I Know My Love* that the male characters are divided between those who deservedly realize their ambitions and those who are left behind to brood over their failures.

The question of economic success is a particularly important one in *Jane* in which the stage directions call for Lord Allan Frobisher, a man who "has discovered that people who have, on their own, achieved the success in life that he has can be overbearing and brutal." In the third act, Mrs. Tower reassures Gilbert Dabney that he possesses "all the attributes of success" since he is "young and attractive and clever." Somewhat later, William Tower echoes the same sentiment when he comforts the aspiring poet Peter Crewe. "I have read all your poems," says Tower, "and I detect something in them that may make you a success."

In *The Worcester Account,* success has a high priority, even though Behrman writes of people whose achievements are ostensibly quite ordinary. Behrman recalls his reading the Horatio Alger

books where "the heros had limited and attainable objectives and
. . . always made them." Because Alger was not distressed by
the perplexing, metaphysical problems that had destroyed Daniel
Asher, Behrman felt that Alger was able to illustrate "that you could
succeed in life without worrying about infinity." Similarly, a reading
of *Duveen* indicates, among other things, that Duveen himself could
not worry over much more than questions of profit and loss. In *The
Burning Glass* Behrman shows that the passion to succeed economically must not interfere with moral responsibilities. In any case,
Brock Dunaway had cynically remarked in *But for Whom Charlie*
that "success is often sheer accident."

II *Money–Marriage–Morality*

Success to Behrman is an amalgam of personal, ethical, and
economic factors. In the second act of *Meteor,* Dr. Avery sum-
marizes the author's view by saying that the secret of success is
wanting something more than anyone else wants it. The observation
was made in chapter 2 that, in Behrman's writing, success is frequently involved with matrimony and that matrimony either promotes or inhibits a man's chances of succeeding in the world. In
some of the plays, as has been made clear, marriage revolves around
economics as much as anything else does. *The Second Man,* of
course, considers candidly the money-marriage question. There is
the suggestion in *Meteor* that Raphael Lord's short-lived financial
empire began partly with his brother-in-law's inheritance, and in
Serena Blandish the only serious matrimonial problem for a poor
girl is money. Accordingly, the poor-girl–rich-boy marriage in *Brief
Moment* has its satiric economic implications. *Biography,* in effect,
illustrates the same thing; for Bunny Nolan's political future hinges
on his contemplated marriage to wealthy Slade Kinnicott.

With the appearance of *End of Summer,* Behrman had added a
new slant to an old theme. Except for the example of Dr. Kenneth
Rice, the fortune-hunting psychiatrist, an abundance of money prevents, rather than promotes, the marriage of Paula Frothingham
and Will Dexter. In *The Talley Method,* however, Dr. Axton Talley
hopes for an economically good marriage arrangement for his son.
When he learns that young Philip is seeing a Greenwich Village
nightclub stripper, he protests vigorously. When Enid Fuller asks
Dr. Talley whether it is not "rather to his credit that [his son]
doesn't want to marry for money," his reply is unequivocal: "it's self

indulgence. It's outrageous." The same sentiment is found in *I Know My Love*, in which Jerome Talbot wants his daughter Emily to marry into all the wealth possible. Of Thomas Chanler, her matrimonial prospect, Talbot cries, "What a background! Not only is Tom's father divorced, but he's bankrupt."

The marital problems in *Jane* are also allied closely with economics. William Tower cannot afford to remarry because his ex-wife preempts most of his income. Mrs. Tower herself comments that her daughter Ann cannot possibly marry Peter Crewe: "he hasn't even got a job. . . . It's high time Ann married and married well." Her remark recalls the sixth chapter of *The Worcester Account* ("Daughter of the Ramaz"), in which the subject is matchmaking and the importance of aligning love and money to good advantage.

Even in such a fundamentally unserious play as the melodramatic *Fanny*, the money-marriage problem is still present. Left pregnant and unwed by Marius, Fanny may as well marry someone wealthy if she is to marry at all. Consequently, the monied Panisse will do very well as a husband until Marius returns from his sea voyage to the widowed Fanny. In *Lord Pengo* there is the example of Mrs. Plumrose Drury, one of Behrman's insufferable provincials, who left a vaudeville act as a young woman to marry a millionaire, only to have the marriage fail utterly. As in so many other instances, money has been the only motive for marriage, but no guarantee exists that it can sustain a relationship.

III *Politics: Left and Right*

Although Behrman passed through a limited Marxist phase prior to 1927, not all of his later work lends itself to a political reading—nor would Behrman regard himself as a political writer in his mature years. International developments in the 1930s and 1940s were too urgent to ignore; and he felt that, up to a point, the condition of humanity should be mirrored in the plays. Had it not been for the political circumstances of the time, the plays might well have been as insulated from the grimness of reality as *The Second Man* and as *Serena Blandish*. The political plays begin with *Meteor* in which Raphael Lord's rise to power symbolizes, in part, the spread of fascism in the world. The more he struggles to preserve his machine-gun utopia, the more he becomes the target of revolutionary movements that seek to undermine him. In other plays, Behrman also portrayed symbolically the Fascist threat to humanity. *Biography*, with its Orrin Kinnicott, contains a dire political warning; and Bunny Nolan is astonished at the thought of Marion Froude's having done portraits of "Communist statesmen." In both *Meteor* and *Biography*, one finds a certain hypersensitivity on the part of Behrman's less tolerant characters toward any kind of even remotely leftist political stance. In *Rain from Heaven*, Hobart Eldridge, like Orrin Kinnicott before him, is an ultraconservative, Communist-fighting, red-white-and-blue champion of the Right.

End of Summer, more than any other play, shows the impact of leftist politics upon the more than comfortably well-to-do. Although Leonie Frothingham is all but totally free from guile, she is the innocent target of her radicalized house guests who envision the possibility of a new social order. Although Behrman remained of a decidedly liberal political cast, he felt uneasy about political polarization. As Hugo Willens says in *Rain from Heaven*, "what security should I have, as a liberal person, if the world goes Communist? Or Fascist?" In the preface to *Wine of Choice*, Behrman cautions that political conviction carried too far becomes dictatorship "and [that] the casualties of such dictatorships are mounting sadly—unhappily even in Russia where so many had pinned their hopes."

Most of the political zealots in the Behrman plays belong to the Right. Dr. Talley is such a person, although he gives the impression that his intertwined professional and political habits are somewhat naive. He, like Pedro Vargas in *The Pirate*, is unusually adept at picking up the scent of anything remotely left-leaning. In act I, Pedro relates his recent history to Serafin, saying that he had come to live in Santa Domingo and had brought his capital with him. "Whose capital?" Serafin asks suspiciously. "My capital," replies Pedro; and he adds, "Are you a communist?" Beneath Pedro's absurd political hypersensitivity, however, Behrman's chief concern is to argue that the forces of political repression should be eliminated. *Jacobowsky and the Colonel* looks with eternal hope that the obstacles inhibiting human freedom will in time be removed. In *Dunnigan's Daughter*, Behrman rejects not only the social vision of the dictatorial entrepreneur Clay Ranier but also that of the Marxist Miguel Riachi. In *I Know My Love*, Jerome Talbot confuses social progress for leftist radicalization. Like Lord Frobisher in *Jane*, Talbot can scarcely envision any progressive social change without attaching a subversive label to it.

IV *Tolerance*

Many of the problems Behrman considers in his writing are related to the toleration of other people and their views. Trouble arises when one person fails to make any effort to listen to, let alone accommodate, other opinions. Clark Storey mentions to Kendall Frayne in the final act of *The Second Man* that she possesses the "two great requirements" for marriage to "a poor but intelligent man: money and tolerance." Lawrence Langner, whose remark about Behrman and tolerance is quite to the point, notes in *The Magic Curtain* that, "after the success of *The Second Man*, Alexander Woollcott scornfully depicted Behrman as a small boy standing outside a stately mansion and peeking in at the windows to learn how life was lived by the upper crust. Woollcott, who peeked into many windows himself, intended his remark to be derisive, but in fact it was complimentary. Had Sam been born in a stately mansion, he might have been blind to the vested injustice and intolerance against which, unlike Woollcott, he wielded his sharpened pen."[1]

Raphael Lord in *Meteor* is what all of Behrman's strong men would continue to be: he is notably lacking in the capacity to abide the views of other people. When the minor character Cass Worthing, "a famous polo player" in *Brief Moment*, objects to Abby Fane's association with a Russian motion-picture director, she appropriately remarks, "How intolerant you are." The problem of tolerance has its greatest emphasis in *Biography* in which three characters are cursed with inflexible minds: Richard Kurt, Bunny Nolan, and Orrin Kinnicott. Kurt, the open enemy of toleration, tells Marion Froude in the second act that, "what you call tolerance I call sloppy laziness." The remark is a key one in the play because tolerance, Marion replies, is her own "essential quality."

In *Rain from Heaven*, Lael Wyngate identifies the "pest" that has overtaken the world as "an epidemic of hatred and intolerance that may engulf us all." Likewise, in *End of Summer*, Behrman provides a house full of people, many of them with seemingly irreconcilable opinions about politics and life who contend with each other continually. Characters like Richard Kurt (*Biography*) and Dow Christophsen (*Wine of Choice*) actively nurture intolerance. Christophsen reminds Ryder Gerrard in act II that "the delights of the world are

an affront because they make tolerable an insupportable world."
He, like Dr. Talley, makes but a few concessions or compromises.
In *Jacobowsky and the Colonel,* the colonel, another character
memorable for his inflexibility, warns Marianne in the second act
that he cannot tolerate being treated with anything less than the
respect to which he feels entitled. In *Dunnigan's Daughter,* Clay
Ranier is either unable or unwilling to listen receptively to any
views which do not originate with him. Behrman's own point of view
is stated in perhaps a more positive way in *Jane* where Peter Crewe
the poet recognizes the necessity of accommodating others, even
the Fascist Lord Frobisher: "I suppose that's the essential difference
between us and the dictators. Even if we disapprove of someone we
allow them to live." William Tower answers, "I congratulate you on
your tolerance, my boy."

In the writing after *Jane,* the word "tolerance" seems to be used
less frequently; but the idea is present. Behrman's prose portraits
were themselves always liberally tolerant; and in *Fanny,* patience
and tolerance, where applied not only to an errant runaway father,
but also to two cantankerous old men, pay rich dividends. *The Cold
Wind and the Warm* is, of course, an overwhelmingly compassionate
play in which human foibles are minimized and in which Behrman
as usual prefers to speculate lovingly upon the deeper, more revealing aspects of his characters. Similarly, Stanley Grant's development in *The Burning Glass* moves toward a more liberal, tolerant
view of the world and its denizens.

V *Jewishness*

Behrman's basic feeling toward Jews and Jewish culture did not
alter much during the productive decades of his career, but it did
undergo a change of emphasis. As chapter 2 indicates, Jews are
scarcely treated at all in the apprenticeship pieces. Not until
Serena Blandish in 1929 did he create a Jewish character, that of
Sigmund Traub, the Bond Street jeweler who uses Serena as a living
manikin. Upon learning of Traub's bargain with Serena, the Countess Flor di Folio immediately senses something shady: "I wager he
capitalises her in some way. Those Jews make money out of everything."

By the mid-1930s, when Behrman was obliged to respond in some
way to Fascist crimes against Jews and others in Europe, he created
the character of Hugo Willens in *Rain from Heaven.* Willens, "a

Nordic with an interesting racial fillip," had been forced to flee
Europe because his grandmother was Jewish. When he discusses
his predicament in "The Chromosome Hunt" story that he relates to
the unsympathetic Hobart Eldridge, he tells of what a "curious
experience" it is to find one's self "a marked person, a special person." In the end, Willens feels that he has no other choice but to
return to Germany: "I must find certitude at last, and, having found
it, if necessary, die for it."

With *Rain from Heaven*, Behrman was coming to terms with
Jewishness. If he himself had become so assimilated into American
life that his Jewishness had begun to erode, the tragedy in
contemporary Europe made it impossible for him to ignore or to
neglect his heritage. Even in *Amphitryon 38* his growing concern
with the problem of modern Jewishness figures. At one point, Alkmena hears Jupiter say that one of "the eleven great beings who will
constitute the finest ornament in all history" shall have a "lovely
Jewish face." *Wine of Choice*, as has been explained, contains the
character of Leo Traub whose description of a pogrom in his native
Lithuanian town parallels in some respects Hugo Willens'
exemplary tale of The Last Jew in *Rain from Heaven*.

Obviously, Behrman later makes much of senseless Jewish persecution. Just as Hobart Eldridge assumes that Willens is a Communist because he is a Jew, Dr. Axton Talley forms the same as-
sumption about the Austrian refugee Manfred Geist in *The Talley
Method*. The wandering Jacobowsky, always the target of anti-
Semitism, says that, although he was born in Poland, that country is
only "the first of my native lands." As late as 1941, paradoxically,
Behrman had thought little about the growing Zionist movement
and the destiny of men like Jacobowsky. Upon hearing Chaim
Weizman speak (see "Zion Comes to Culver City" in *Chaim Weizman*), the urgency of modern Jewishness dawned on him rather
suddenly: "If the Nazis won the war there would no longer be a
Jewish problem. The Nazis would have settled it in their own way.
But he [Weizman] was sure they would not win it. . . . Even so;
what would be the position of those millions of Jews—what would
be left of them—living now in a limbo that was neither death nor
life?"

After the war, Behrman's feeling toward Jewish life and culture
became decreasingly alarmist and increasingly ardent. *The Worcester Account* and its dramatic adaptation, *The Cold Wind and the*

Warm, reveal some remarkable insights about the Jewish experience in America. *Duveen*, of course, is also a Jewish portrait; but Behrman somehow chose not to emphasize that aspect of his subject; and in *Lord Pengo*, the dramatic adaptation of *Duveen*, the same treatment exists. In the second act, however, Behrman has Pengo strive to interest his client Enoch Drury in Masaccio's "The Circumcision"; but Drury protests: "I am not in Jewish rites." Pengo is characteristically both comprehending and tactful: "Not at all. I understand prejudice." A similar detail appears in *But for Whom Charlie* where it becomes known that Seymour Rosenthal had once been excluded from a college fraternity because he was a Jew. *The Burning Glass*, with its stress on the acceptance of Jewish identity, forms the final link in Behrman's lengthy commentary on the dilemma of modern Jewishness.

VI *Friendship*

Ultimately, Behrman's thoughts lead toward the ideal of interpersonal harmony with tolerance and without prejudice. When his characters are at their best, they enjoy the rewards of friendship and mutual involvement. In the final act of *Amphitryon 38*, Jupiter and Alkmena are gradually coming to terms with each other, and the subject turns to friendship. "What is its object?" Jupiter asks. Alkmena's reply is crucial to the understanding of S. N. Behrman: "To bring together the most totally dissimilar people and make them equal. Have you never seen the most ill-assorted creatures isolate themselves for no reason at all? A cabinet minister and a gardener—a lion sharing his cage with a poodle? And these misfits have a perfect community of interests—they seem drawn together by some strange, chemical substance in their bodies."

More often than not, however, Behrman's dissimilar people are not mutually attracted but tend to clash sharply. The conflicts that originate over differences in philosophy, politics, and personality are many in Behrman's characters; but the strong bonds of friendship that link some of his characters are of special significance. Marion Froude's relationship with Melchior Feydak in *Biography* is grounded on mutual trust and admiration; these two are the only fully tolerant people on stage, and their ability to tolerate is partly the reason for their satisfying friendship.

Lael Wyngate in *Rain from Heaven* is a strong friendship advocate. When Hugo Willens facetiously tells her that "friendship is relative—a thermometer of expediency," she does not appreciate his cynicism: "It's like pressing a drop of blood on a slide and saying: 'This is the stuff that flows in your veins!' It isn't, though. When it's in your veins it's something different." Behrman's attitude toward his biographical subjects—consistently warm and enthusiastic—is his attitude toward the human race in general. His portrait of Max Beerbohm probably evinces more affection than any of his other biographical pieces, but the impact of Behrman's relationship with confidant Daniel Asher is central to an understanding of *The Worcester Account* and *The Cold Wind and the Warm*. Stanley Grant's close connection with his older friend and adviser Alexander Löwe in *The Burning Glass* has particular significance in the novel, for Löwe pilots Grant on the road to self-discovery.

Thus, while it is highly desirable to maintain an open, tolerant mind, it is especially necessary, Behrman indicates, to create deeper avenues of understanding through the medium of friendship. His strong men, his political and philosophical zealots, are those who have denied friendship and have replaced it with self-centeredness and monomania. Raphael Lord (*Meteor*), Dr. Kenneth Rice (*End of Summer*), and Dr. Axton Talley (*The Talley Method*), to cite only three examples, are spiritually destroyed because they find it impossible to form genuine human attachments.

VII   *The Generations*

One of the chief reasons that Behrman's characters often fail to exist in harmony with each other is the difference brought about by age. Especially in the plays, as had been noted, a certain uneasiness prevails between the generations. Characteristically, Behrman sides with his older, more mature characters as a general rule. His preference in *The Second Man* is for Kendall Frayne and not for the younger, craftier Monica Grey. But preferences aside, conflict frequently exists between the younger characters and their seniors; in fact, the strain arises often from a feeling of inferiority and inadequacy in the young. Douglas Carr in *Meteor* regards himself as "just another dull son of a brilliant father." The anonymous young man who appears in the opening scene of *Serena Blandish* leaves Serena with the luncheon check to pay, and the person who finally pays the bill is Sigmund Traub, the middle-aged Jewish gentleman. In the same play, conflict occurs between the butler Martin and his son Edgar Mallison; and, in *Brief Moment*, Roderick Dean harbors a special resentment toward his father. The conflict that arises between Orrin Kinnicott and his daughter Slade (*Biography*), as well as the conflict between Marion Froude and Richard Kurt, is caused partly, if not mainly, by the difference in their ages. Joan Eldridge (*Rain from Heaven*) does not share her father's views because, as she cries in frustration, "He's so damned cautious!"

The amiable conflict that develops between Mrs. Wyler and Will Dexter at the opening of *End of Summer* contains the old woman's gentle rebuke: "Do you think your generation has a monopoly on hard times?" Later, a remark by Leonie Frothingham brings the generation question into better focus when she avers that "one generation never has any perspective about another." In the first act of the play, she discusses her daughter Paula with her ex-husband Sam Frothingham:

LEONIE: Well, when I was a child I was brought up to care only if people were charming or attractive or . . .
SAM: Well-connected . . .
LEONIE: Yes . . . These kids don't care a hoot about that.
SAM: I think the difference between their generation and ours is that we were romantic and they're realistic.
LEONIE: Is that it?
SAM: I think so.
LEONIE: What makes that?
SAM: Changes in the world—the war—the depression.

The prologue to *Amphitryon 38* reveals a difference in point of view between Jupiter and his half-son Mercury, just as Dow Christophsen's views clash sharply with those of his elders in *Wine of Choice*. Philo Smith, the financier in *No Time for Comedy*, reveals to Linda Esterbrook that he has been alienated from his Socialist son at Harvard. Dr. Talley has a similar problem: "Each generation has to justify itself," he counsels Enid Fuller in the final scene. Dr. Talley has managed to destroy his son's spirit by reminding him that he has somehow not succeeded in justifying himself. In *Dunnigan's Daughter*, Clay Ranier tells his wife that he has had trouble squaring his values with those of his father whom he regards as "a tyrannical man, a hypocrite hiding behind a façade of religion." *I Know My Love* contains a considerable amount of generation conflict. In *Fanny*, trouble breaks out between Marius and his father as well as between Fanny and her mother. Regarding Fanny's child, Marius asks Cesar, "who is the father, the one who gives life or the one who buys the bibs?" Cesar replies, "the father is the one who loves." A story called "The History of the Russian Revolution" which Behrman published in *The New Yorker* on November 24, 1956 has mostly to do with the conflict between father and son—the former, a liberal; the latter, a radical. When the father throws his hands up in disgust, a friend tries to comfort the old man by asking, "who could understand young people nowadays?"

Often little or no love exists between the fathers and sons in Behrman's plays. The unhappy arrangement results from the failure of the son to meet the expectations of the father. Walter Cannon Brink III in *Lord Pengo* regards his son as "a great disappointment." Later in the play, Pengo and his artist son Derek part after a stormy exchange of angry rhetoric. Reminiscent of *Brief Moment* and *The Talley Method*, Derek intends to marry his model, partly, no doubt, to spite his father. The unsatisfactory father-son relationships are again present in Behrman's final play, *But for Whom Charlie*, when it becomes known that, as a child, Willard Prosper vowed to kill his father.

VIII *The Comic Vision*

Despite considerations of such conflicts, Behrman indicates often that, beyond a certain point, it is a mistake to view life too seriously. "Sad thing about geniuses," Clark Storey muses at the beginning of *The Second Man*, "[they] almost invariably lack humor." At the end of the play, he tells Monica Grey that "life is sad" but that "it's gallant—to pretend that it isn't." While most of Behrman's lines are not altogether comic in the usual sense of the term, he strove in much of what he wrote to demonstrate that one must view life in a positive, even a comic, way. Some characters, on the other hand, suffer in life because they are deficient in the comic, affirmative point of view.

In *Meteor*, Ann Carr correctly notes that what passes for humor in Raphael Lord is in reality "condescension." Richard Kurt (*Biography*) fails to see the positive, constructive benefits of humor. He applies what little sense of humor he has to cynical derision: "I want to reduce the whole system to absurdity. I want to laugh the powers that be out of existence." Kurt is similar to Hobart Eldridge, who concedes at the end of *Rain from Heaven* that his "sense of humor is defective." Lael Wyngate answers, "Too bad. I wonder what we can do about it."

One of the tasks that challenges the characters in the plays is the maintenance of the comic vision of life, especially when it appears that life should be read in tragic terms. Binkie Niebuhr poses a question in *Wine of Choice* which is never answered: "Why is it that as they grow older professional humorists get more and more bitter?" This question appears again in *No Time for Comedy* when Gay Esterbrook temporarily loses touch with the comic vein, except that here his wife aids him in recovering it. Jacobowsky also, finds that to endure life one must nurture the comic, positive point of view. The essays that Behrman wrote from wartime London show that without an affirmative frame of mind the British might not have maintained their equilibrium under the impossible circumstances imposed by the German bombing. Emily Chanler in *I Know My Love* reminds her brother-in-law that much of life can be regarded only as a joke and that "we must be prepared to laugh, even when the joke is on ourselves."

In a 1952 interview with *The New York Times*, Behrman articulated his idea of the comic vision more precisely. "The essense of the comic sense," he said, "is awareness: awareness of the tragedy as well as the fun of life, of the pity, the futility, the lost hopes, the striving for immortality, for permanence, for security, for love." He continued, "for laughter is the most humanizing—as well as the most critical—agency in the world."[2] Behrman appears himself to be what he called his character Melchior Feydak in *Biography*: "a humorist with a rather sad face."

IX *Minor Aspects*

Besides these major concerns, Behrman's plays contain certain secondary thematic aspects that deserve mention. To examine the plays is to become aware, for example, that Behrman reacts negatively to social drinking, physical culture, and newspapers. The only function that alcohol serves in the plays is to loosen tongues, intensify emotions, and befuddle minds. In *The Second Man*, Austin Lowe is motivated by alcohol to fire a gun at Clark Storey (and to miss his mark). In *Brief Moment*, in which a good deal of imbibing goes on, Abby Fane warns Cass Worthing that drinking brings out his least attractive side; and the worst of Hobart Eldridge is revealed in the final act of *Rain from Heaven* where Behrman has him drinking heavily. Linda Esterbrook regretfully remarks in *No Time for Comedy* that when her playwright husband is "between ideas he makes an alcoholic tour of the town." Dr. Talley in *The Talley*

Method advises Enid Fuller against drinking: "cocktails are not particularly good for you." Clay Ranier in *Dunnigan's Daughter*, who has received the same advice, follows his doctor's prohibitions about food but not about drink. The unstable Daniel Talbot (*I Know My Love*) conceals what he calls his "mounting sense of inadequacy" by drinking to excess; and, in *Jane*, William Tower accuses Lord Frobisher of evading reality by turning to books, music, fantasy, and alcohol. Escartifique in *Fanny* is able to speak his mind to Panisse only when he is "drunk enough," and young Willard Prosper in *But for Whom Charlie* is prevented from confronting his personal problems directly because of his struggles with alcohol.

Behrman's cynicism toward athletes and physical culturists is a probable reflection of his own dislike for the strenuous, sporting life and of the fiasco he made of the "physical education" obligation at Clark College. In the plays, physical strength is an ironic symbol of spiritual and even of physical weakness. Sherman Maxwell, the "all-American end of great renown" in *Meteor*, is an intolerant mesomorph who perishes of "football heart" at the conclusion of the first act. Orrin Kinnicott in *Biography* is described as one who "makes a fetish of exercise" and who has appeared in health magazines clad only in his underwear. Hobart Eldridge's dream of a fascist "American Youth League" in *Rain from Heaven* involves finding young men "interested in physical culture." In *End of Summer*, Will Dexter speaks deprecatingly of the undergraduate world of football and Reserve Officer's Training Corps. Allan Frobisher in *Jane*, predictably enough, is another health and physical culture faddist. William Tower says in the first act of the play that Frobisher had once displayed himself "stark naked" at a swimming pool before "a highly respectable American lady novelist." The minor character Dan Eisner in *The Cold Wind and the Warm*, while he appears to be robust and healthy, dies during the course of the play from diabetes.

Perhaps Behrman's stint as a journalist during the lean years in New York caused him to have a lifelong distrust for newspapers and their publishers, and in his plays newspapers are never spoken of with anything but suspicion. Raphael Lord calls the press "yellow" in *Meteor*, and Roderick Dean finds it curious in *Brief Moment* that understatement ever appears in the pages of a newspaper. *Biography* concerns in part a conspiracy to control the news media, and in it the first of Behrman's right-wing newspaper owners (Orrin Kinnicott) appears. In *Rain from Heaven*, there is apparently another attempt to control the press, and in *End of Summer* the pet project among the young radicals is the creation of a leftist magazine representing the National Student Federation. In *Wine of Choice*, Ryder Gerrard owns a newspaper in his home state of New Mexico; and he uses the press to advance his own political interests. References to newspapers in *No Time for Comedy* reveal them as mere outlets for the dissemination of details on divorces, scandals, and sensations of all kinds. Early in *The Talley Method* Behrman identifies newspapers with deliberate whitewashing, for Cy Blodgett brandishes the latest edition of the daily paper which contains a "cold and statistical" article which reassures the readership "that there is no unemployment in America." Jerome Talbot in *I Know My Love* objects to his daughter's seeing "a cheap newspaper scribbler" who has written in favor of reducing the working day to thirteen hours. It is Allen Frobisher (*Jane*) who controls a chain of "grubby newspapers." In *Lord Pengo* one of the better culture customers is the mysterious Cosmo Prince, who is called "the most important press lord in America."

CHAPTER 7

Matters of Technique

S. N. BEHRMAN has been labeled variously as a writer of "high comedy," "comedy of manners," "sophisticated comedy," "drawing-room comedy," "comedy of illumination," and "polite comedy." Whether or not these designations are precisely definable, they are not particularly distinguishable. Undeniably, however, the popularity of Behrman's plays was in large part attributable to his refined comic sense. His three longest-running plays—*Fanny, Jacobowsky and the Colonel*, and *I Know My Love*—were no doubt successes at the box office because of the way they treated problems with a certain comic-intelligence. For example, Panisse, who is about to die in the final act of *Fanny*, ruminates on what he will miss most in life, and says that it is the little pleasures such as lunch and dinner. In the first act of *Jacobowsky*, the protagonist himself risks the falling bombs from Hitler's army to leave his hotel for a supply of *marrons glacés*. Finally, in the first act of *I Know My Love*, Thomas Chanler reads aloud a review of a book called "The World and the Individual" by a certain Professor Royce: "This conglomeration of vapors," Chanler reads, "is called 'The World and the Individual.' It need only be said of this effusion . . . that it serves to demonstrate that the author's knowledge of the world is as fragmentary as his intuition about the individual is opaque."

The cleverness of such lines as these undoubtedly held an appeal for a certain kind of playgoer, one whose comic sense had been honed to a finer than usual edge. Moreover, this particular kind of comic appeal is undoubtedly a reflection of the comic quality to be found in the two plays that Behrman himself admired the most: Oscar Wilde's *The Importance of Being Earnest* and Noel Coward's *Blithe Spirit*.[1] Certain other playwrights, notably Somerset Maugham and George Bernard Shaw, had long attracted his admiration; and Behrman belongs temperamentally, as well as aesthetically, among these playwrights, whose closest American parallel he became. There were few other high-comedy writers in America. "For a time," Behrman wrote recently, "Philip Barry, Arthur Richman, Paul Osborn, and I were the only American writers of high comedy."[2] But, in America, the rhetorical characteristics of Behrman's plays have never been seriously rivaled, and his skill in the essay has been equaled by few.

Although his plays differ somewhat in their manner of presentation over the years, certain aspects of the Behrman style remain constant. His audiences came to the theater anticipating rapid, articulate dialogue punctuated by deft ironic exchanges and wry innuendo. In act II of *Jane,* for example, Gilbert Dabney sorts through a series of social invitations with Jane Fowler:

GILBERT: By the way, Jane, we have to decide about the week-end. We have four invitations already.
JANE: Gilbert can never resist an invitation.
GILBERT: No. I'd like to accept them all. Here's one from Lord Duffield.
JANE: That's horses.
GILBERT: How do you get on with the horsey set?
JANE: They're rather simple. I talk to them about easy books and I pass for an intellectual.
GILBERT: Anson Dykes wants us too.
TOWER: The effervescent historian. How do you get on with him, Jane?
JANE: I simply let him bubble. He is dazzled with his own identity.
GILBERT: Anson's crazy about Jane. He's dedicating his new book to her. He tells everybody she's brilliant.
JANE: He thinks me brilliant because I never interrupt him.

Part of the comic effect comes no doubt from the speed with which the remarks flow. Although not all the plays were well received, Behrman never lost his sense of the rhetorical pace evident in these lines from *Jane.*

Behrman also remained at least mildly satiric, more so in his plays than in his essays. Behrman characters, unless they are too young, are polite and diplomatic on the surface. They are witty when they are at their best; at their worst, they are impossibly glib. Their discourse is characterized by its crispness, its civility, and its personal and anecdotal quality. Behrman's theatrical language, like the language of his essays, is richly modulated, balanced, and resourceful in its color and variety. Behrman tells in *People in a Diary,* for example, of Arnold Bennett's reaction to *Serena Blandish:* "I saw

your play last night. The first act was all right, but then we both
know it isn't hard to write a good first act. The second I thought fell
off a bit, and I was q-q-q-quite p-p-p-pleased. But the third came
back a bit and I was quite a-a-a-annoyed."

I *Character Names*

S. N. Behrman not infrequently gives his characters representa-
tional names. It is not by chance, for instance, that the writer-
protagonist of *The Second Man* is named "Storey," or that his
psychologically depressed companion bears the name "Lowe." As
has been noted before, Storey's first name (Clark) may have been
prompted by Behrman's mental association with Clark College. In
Meteor, the name "Raphael Lord" is a pseudonym intended to stress
that character's godlike, indomitable self-image. In a similar way,
Serena Blandish's name seems to denote serenity and flattery; and,
among her matrimonial prospects, centenarian Sir Everard Pyncheon is a man with a faintly comic-obscene name; and the same
might be said about another of her pursuers, Lord Ivor Cream. The
feminine lead in *Brief Moment* (Abby Fane) bears a name that
suggests "feign" as well as "profane"; her first name, however, may
relate to her being called "that nun-like creature" in act III.

Elsewhere in the plays, one finds characters like Richard Kurt
(*Biography*) whose name easily befits his curt manner. Marion
Froude's name in the context of that play invites the association
of "Freud" and "prude." In *End of Summer*, young Will Dexter's
name appropriately suggests "dexterous"; and his elderly friend Mrs.
Wyler, who represents a bygone age of free-wheeling capitalism,
possesses a name that alludes to her craftiness. Makepeace
Lovell, a name not unlike that of a Restoration-comedy character,
fulfills his role as peacemaker and reconciler in *No Time for
Comedy*.

The Raniers of *Dunnigan's Daughter* are economically lofty and
powerful in much the same sense that the Towers in *Jane* represent
high social position. In *Fanny*, Marius's "mistress" of the sea is a
square rigger appropriately christened the *Malaisie*, which aptly
symbolizes his own moral quandary. *The Cold Wind and the Warm*
contains the character Rappaport (a matchmaker), and Behrman's
fictional name for himself in the play is Tobey Sacher, around whom
the past hangs like "a heavy sack." The name "Pengo" in *Lord Pengo*
denotes a Hungarian coin. One of Pengo's clients, Walter Cannon

Brink III, also bears a name identified with money. *But for Whom Charlie* contains the Prospers—Faith, Willard and Gillian—who, ironically, prosper but little in the play.

II *Character Types*

The preceding chapters have included comment about certain characters and character types that reappear in a succession of plays and that hold essentially the same philosophical and temperamental characteristics. One of these designations is the "strong man," which includes characters like Raphael Lord, Orrin Kinnicott, Hobart Eldridge, Dr. Kenneth Rice, Dr. Axton Talley, Allan Frobisher, and Lord Pengo. Aside from whatever differences that exist between them, they all share a certain overwhelmingly dictatorial and profoundly inflexible quality that is a part not only of their personality but also of their invariably right-wing political inclinations. Behrman used this kind of character on so many occasions to represent the hard-headed resistance to toleration and accommodation on a personal as well as a political level. He used this character "type" as a contrast to certain of his women who become, as has been shown, the pivot of attention in the plays and who represent unfailing good sense, emotional maturity, and tolerant understanding of human values: Kendall Frayne, Serena Blandish, Abby Fane, Marion Froude, Lael Wyngate, Leonie Frothingham (to a limited extent), Linda Esterbrook, Enid Fuller, Fern Dunnigan, and Emily Chanler. In the midst of the crowd, Behrman places characters with real or supposed Marxist leanings who spice the conversations: Dennis McCarthy, Dow Christophsen, Avis Talley, and Miguel Riachi.

Most of the artists and writers in Behrman's plays are sophisticated worldlings who are notably less than first-class artists, a handicap they are ruefully forced to acknowledge. Clark Storey in *The Second Man* is a "second-rate" writer, for example; and other subsequent characters who have the same problem are Edgar Mallison, the Stranger (*Serena Blandish*); Roderick Dean, Melchior Feydak, Marion Froude, Warwick Wilson (*Biography*); Sasha Barashaev, Miguel Riachi, Daniel Chanler (*I Know My Love*); Peter Crewe, William Tower, Aaron (*The Cold Wind and the Warm*); Derek Pengo, and Willard Prosper. Occasionally what Behrman's artists lack in artistic successfulness they compensate for in personal attractiveness, as Marion Froude does.

The same cannot be said, however, about his scientists. Austin Lowe, referred to in *The Second Man* as a first-rate scientist, is decent but insufferably dull. Dr. Kenneth Rice in *End of Summer* is a successful psychiatrist but also an opportunistic scoundrel. Dr. Axton Talley, also a very successful physician, is described as a man who "can't see beyond the end of his duodenum." Willie Lavin, regarded by Tobey Sacher as a scientist in *The Cold Wind and the Warm*, suffers from a hopeless mental maladjustment and ends his life in suicide, while in the same play the family physician Dr. Nightingale can do no better than express a cynical optimism.

III *Setting*

The handsome settings of Behrman's plays, many of them designed by Jo Mielziner, are another expression of Behrman's fascination with prosperity and cultural elegance; and yet not all of the plays, in fact, demand elegant sets. *Biography, The Pirate, Jacobowsky and the Colonel* and *The Cold Wind and the Warm*, for example, do not call for lush surroundings. Other plays, especially *Serena Blandish, Meteor*, and *Fanny*, make use of strong contrasts in setting; for the characters move from poverty to privilege. Characters in these plays, while not particularly monied (at least initially), still have expensive tastes.

Behrman's American settings are all located on the eastern seaboard. There are no instances in which a play is set in the South or West, and Behrman's disdain for the American provinces prompted him to refer with a certain condescension to any part of America other than New York or New England. That five plays are set either in England or France is one more indication that his cultural orientation was decidedly more cosmopolitan than narrowly American. He says in his memoirs, for example, that he had always had "a nostalgia for England" and a keen interest in the English literary scene. He always used "foreign" characters not only in his plays but also in his essays and fiction, thereby helping to create a more cosmopolitan atmosphere. The usual scene in a Behrman play is a studio apartment or living room. His civilized characters fit best in a civilized setting; therefore, the people harmonize well with their surroundings.

IV *Structure*

One of the most often voiced negative criticisms of Behrman plays has always been their paucity of clear structural form and their failure to achieve much in the way of dramatic progression. Such criticism is justified, for too often too many characters are engaged in too much apparently directionless chatter. The organic connection between character, dialogue, and them is at least occasionally unclear, as for example in *Wine of Choice*. In the lesser plays especially, the audience is left without much of a key to the perplexities that the play introduces. There seems surely to be the implied faith in Behrman plays that, ultimately, political and moral crises will find a way of resolving themselves. In the end, Behrman implies, common sense, rationality, and truth will prevail over the forces of evil and darkness. But even so, as is made rather clear in such plays as *Meteor, End of Summer, Jacobowsky and the Colonel,* and *Lord Pengo,* the best can only be hoped for because the problems raised are still unresolved in the end.

Structurally, Behrman's plays neither develop nor end; they begin *in medias res* and conclude with a sometimes pleasantly oblique or ironic line later in the evening. Maurice Zolotow has correctly pointed out that "Behrman was as awkward at plot construction as he was smooth at dialogue and characters."[3] The easy, lucid, organic progression of story line was, in fact, a characteristic that Behrman never mastered—or perhaps never had an interest in mastering. *The Second Man,* Behrman's first successful play, remains as his best-constructed play, if only because he observes the unities of time, place, and action. The elapsed time of the play extends from late one afternoon until the following morning. The place is Clark Storey's apartment on West Fifty-sixth Street in New York, and the action centers around Clark Storey's problems with money and matrimony. Little, if anything, in the play is extraneous; but such is not the case with the other plays.

Zolotow's account of the Boston rehearsal of *Meteor,* for example, is interesting for the light it casts on Behrman's artistic priorities as well as on the somewhat inconclusive character of the play. Behrman had originally written *Meteor* in four acts. According to Zolotow, director Philip Moeller could not resist the urge to rewrite the script into three acts with increased emphasis on structure rather than on character. The result was a series of spirited arguments between Moeller, Behrman, and the principal actors.[4] Behrman, unable to tolerate Moeller, stalked out of the theater; but, with the house sold out, the play had to go on as scheduled. Zolotow quotes Lunt as saying that, "with an opening night to face," he had been left with nothing to say on the telephone in the play's final scene. Eventually, Lunt is alleged to have said that "Berri wrote us an ending, though the play never really had an ending even in New York."[5]

The reasons for this formlessness in Behrman's plays is a matter of conjecture. There is no record, for example, of Behrman's ever having responded to the criticism about the structural looseness of his plays. The impression gained from a thorough reading of Behrman's dramas and essays tends to support the view that Behrman sees the universe around him as being essentially unordered and without beginning or end. Not one of his plays is altogether conclusive in the sense that all its issues are settled; instead, Behrman seems to recreate scenes from life rather than to recognize any huge cosmic patterns in it. He is concerned instead with tangible human problems that affect life in the short run, such as have been discussed earlier: marriage, intolerance, unbridled ambition, and political tyranny.

V *Psychology*

W. David Sievers has written that "Behrman's contribution to the psycho-analytic drama ranks in importance with that of O'Neill and Barry" and that Behrman "typifies the post-Freudian playwrights of the thirties who directed their psychoanalytically sharpened observations away from the individual in isolation and toward the socio-centered problems of fascism, radicalism, racial intolerance and greed, which are best understood in terms of the unconscious pressures causing them."[6] Siever's pronouncement seems surely to overstate the importance of the overt use of psychology in Behrman's plays.

Behrman was, as has been made clear, reasonably aware of the principles of modern psychology, having studied under G. Stanley Hall at Clark College. He had, in fact, authored, in 1914, an ambitious undergraduate essay entitled "Psychology and the New Philosophy of the Theatre" for *The Clark College Monthly*. He had some acquaintance with Freudian psychology; he had heard Freud's Worcester address in 1909; and Sievers quotes Behrman as stating that "I have lived . . . in an atmosphere where most of my friends were undergoing psychoanalysis, and I have had long and exhausting talks with practitioners."[7]

Nonetheless, Behrman remained leery of taking psychology too seriously. Certain of his characters—such as Raphael Lord; Dr. Kenneth Rice, the psychiatrist; Dr. Axton Talley; and Willie Lavin—might well be considered from a critical position as informed about modern psychoanalysis; but the bulk of Behrman's writing does not lend itself particularly to a psychological reading. Although allusions to Freud, psychology, and psychoanalysis occur in his writing, little evidence exists that such references are anything more than casual in significance. The playgoer is exposed to Monica Grey's "Freudian patter" in *The Second Man*, and in *Meteor* psychology enters the conversation in a superficial way. In *Serena Blandish*, Martin makes the comment that success "is hidden in the byways of psychology"; and, in *Brief Moment*, Harold Sigrift remarks that psychoanalysis "makes quite simple people feel they're complex."

Feydak's opinion of psychology in *Biography* is in the same suspicious vein. "The new psychology," he tells Marion Froude, "is very confusing." He continues, "in my simple day you said: 'That young man is bumptious and insufferable' and you dismissed him. Now you say: 'He has an inferiority complex' and you encourage him to be more bumptious and insufferable." Lael Wyngate speaks of psychology in a similar way in *Rain from Heaven:* "Don't you think . . . that the subconscious has been done to death and that it's high time someone re-discovered the conscious?" Dennis McCarthy in *End of Summer* wonders about the "Great Pan Sexualist of Vienna" and speculates about "who analysed Sig Freud himself." Ryder Gerrard, upon first meeting young Dow Christophsen (*Wine of Choice*), finds him to be "a rather Mephistophelian angel, well dipped in Freud."

Behrman has Enid Fuller (*The Talley Method*) say that, in spite of all her personal problems, she cannot abide "the endless career of audible introspection" that psychoanalysis seems to bring with it. Jacobowsky, in one of Behrman's funnier lines, says that the only use to which an understanding of abnormal psychology might be put is to better get along with one's relatives. In *Dunnigan's Daughter*, Zelda Ranier recognizes that one of Miguel Riachi's strongest points is that "he psychoanalyzes you without making you lie down." Finally, in *The Cold Wind and the Warm*, Behrman reduces psychology to absurdity in the scene in which Willie Lavin and Myra are conversing on the piazza in the rain:

MYRA: I know it's silly. Why is it? Why am I so scared?

WILLIE: (*Cracks his knuckles*) I venture to say that if you analyzed it to its source you'd find some deep psychic . . .

MYRA: (*Interrupts him*) Willie, why do you crack your knuckles like that? You're always doing it. Why?

WILLIE: (*Turning it off adroitly*) Perhaps for the same reason you're afraid of thunder.

(*They both laugh a little*)

CHAPTER 8

Perspectives

S. N. BEHRMAN differs in certain important respects from most American writers of his generation. His literary upbringing was initially an academic one, and the works he was destined to write tend to reflect the subtle influences of having had a fairly structured exposure to literature in the classrooms of Clark, Harvard, and Columbia in the second decade of the twentieth century. Had it not been for the fortunate and determined intervention of his friend Daniel Asher, Behrman might well have accepted a teaching appointment at the University of Minnesota in 1918, succumbed to the comfortable respectability of academic life, and written little or nothing of consequence afterward. As it happened, however, Behrman used his literary education as a vast creative and civilizing resource that shaped his *weltanschauung* and provided him a place in the literature of modern America.

I *The Heritage*

As early as 1939, Joseph Wood Krutch recognized that Behrman had secured for himself "as sure a position in the contemporary American theater as any writer can claim";[1] and in 1952 John Gassner, writing appreciatively of Behrman, called him "the only remaining writer of high comedy . . . [and] perhaps the only consistently brilliant stylist in our drama."[2] Such praise is high and deserving, but the vicissitudes of literary fame are fickle. When Jay B. Hubble's *Who Are the Major American Writers?* was published by the Duke University Press in 1972, Behrman's name was not among the legions of writers mentioned. Because Behrman survives as a dramatist and as a prose writer of considerable stature, his omission is a regrettable oversight, for Behrman can easily be placed within the mainstream of American letters. His relationship with other playwrights aside, Behrman shares a number of characteristics in

common with another New Englander, Nathaniel Hawthorne. Like
Hawthorne, he has a gnawing preoccupation with moral problems,
as is quite apparent in such plays as *Meteor, Jane* and *Lord Pengo*
where he raises ethical questions about money and matrimony. He
also shares with Hawthorne a markedly suspicious attitude toward
modern science, as is evidenced in *The Second Man* and in *The
Talley Method.* Skepticism toward social reformers (*End of Summer*)
and Oedipal conflicts between parents and children (*Lord Pengo,
But for Whom Charlie*) are themes also found in Hawthorne's works.

In common with the arch-cosmopolitan Henry James, Behrman
possesses an almost instinctive repugnance toward American vulgar-
ity and narrow provincialism, both of which he treats in *Duveen;*
but, in spite of this attitude, he maintained a certain mannered,
polished, subtly humorous, and yet humanistic vision of the world
and its people. Behrman's characters, like those of Henry James, are
frequently unfettered by matrimony and have names that are highly
indicative, if not outrightly allegorical. Behrman's characters, such
as Clark Storey and Lael Wyngate, seem to postpone certain critical
decisions about the destiny of their lives until it is too late, just as
the characters in Henry James's fiction often do. Like James,
Behrman is a limited social realist with a special awareness of, and
appreciation for, the psychological implications of human behavior.
It is with a certain wry detachment that Behrman, along with James,
treats life in the upper economic (if not social) classes that are closely
identified with modern urban life along the eastern seaboard and in
Europe. Consistent with Hawthorne and James, Behrman has but
little feeling for nature in her primal state. Obviously no Agrarian,
Behrman's world is the world of streets and buildings, restaurants
and living rooms. For him, nature is as removed from his conscious-
ness as the remote and dimly conceptualized American provinces to
which he occasionally alludes.

As a young writer of short fiction particularly in the pages of *The
Smart Set,* Behrman obviously patterned himself after the American
realists such as Howells, Norris, and Dreiser, who harbored serious
reservations about the American Dream; and Behrman's early fiction embraced the familiar tendencies associated with turn of the
century realism: deprived characters, leftist politics, and a threaten-
ingly competitive economic system. In his later, more established
drama and prose essays, it is possible to see Behrman in the context
of American Jewish writers, especially after he gradually devoted

more attention to the dilemmas of Jewish life posed by the rise of fascism in the 1930s. Although he seldom used a Yiddish or Hebrew phrase, or infrequently relied on anything approaching ethnic humor, certain aspects of the Jewish experience found their way into his writing beginning with *Serena Blandish* (1929).

The Worcester Account, which deals in part with Jewish life in America, contains echoes of an ostensibly very different sort of Jewish book, Abraham Cahan's novel *The Rise of David Levinsky* (1917), which it resembles both in content and in style. In each book there is treatment of the problems inherent in maintaining the Jewish identity in America and in rising economically. Like Behrman himself, the fictional hero of Cahan's novel can scarcely comprehend, and is amazed by, the forces that have rescued him from poverty and anonymity. Levinsky's words toward the opening of the novel are curiously parallel to Behrman's attitude toward himself: "sometimes, when I think of my past in a superficial, casual way, the metamorphosis I have gone through strikes me as nothing short of a miracle. I was born and reared in the lowest depths of poverty and I arrived in America—in 1885—with four cents in my pocket. I am now worth more than two million dollars. . . ."

Like Cahan and the whole tradition of Jewish writers in America, Behrman writes primarily of the city. His enlightened liberal political views, his penchant for analyzing the moral consequences of everyday acts and gestures, and his occasional reference to Jewish social and religious rituals are not so different in character from the writing of such younger American Jews as Bernard Malamud and Saul Bellow. As has been explained, however, Behrman, for reasons of his own, occasionally avoided identification with both Jewishness and Americaness in the early years of his literary career.

It has also been noted that the flavor of Behrman's theatrical comedy is closest to playwrights like Shaw, Coward, and Maugham, although in America his closest resemblence is to Philip Barry. Unlike most playwrights, however, Behrman designed plays that he believed would bring out the best in his favorite players: the Lunts, Alexander Woollcott, Ina Claire, Lawrence Olivier, and others. These were performers who, in one sense or another, were best able to infuse life into a Behrman script. It is therefore understandable that Behrman wrote plays around living actors, inasmuch as two of his chief concerns were with people and with theatrical success.

As an essayist, Behrman owes much to those other magnificent essayists of his time who, like himself, contributed to *The New Yorker:* James Thurber, E. B. White, and S. J. Perelman. It was the combined influence of such persons that created and nurtured *The New Yorker* prose style, a style characterized in part by its urbane, intelligent, and subtle appeal to a sophisticated audience. Indeed, Behrman's own prose style is at times scarcely distinguishable from that of his peers.

II   *The Writer in Retrospect*

As for an assessment of Behrman in his own right, considered apart from those literary influences that were brought to bear on him, there is the inescapable conclusion that some of his plays and published books were a critical success; some were not. Only his prose essays remained at a high level of achievement and survive today as the best of his work. His one attempt at writing a novel, as has been made clear, was, by common consensus and by his own estimation, a failure. In truth, the often commended brilliance of his stage dialogues has been overstressed through the years by friendly critics such as Joseph Wood Krutch. It required, after all, such theatrical talent as that of the Lunts, Katherine Cornell, and Ina Claire to bring Behrman his stage successes, although not infrequently the discontentment of his principal actors sent Behrman back to his desk for the revision of an entire scene. Too often, however, no amount of rewriting would save certain plays such as *Wine of Choice* and *Dunnigan's Daughter* from the deserved wrath of critics.

Probably the most astute assessment of Behrman is that of John Gassner who wrote that "Behrman's art of comedy, including his so-called comic detachment consists of an ambivalence of attitudes that has as its sources the simultaneous possession of a nimble mind and a mellow temperament."[3] For Behrman is at the same time critical and forgiving of human weakness. The "nimble mind" of which Gassner speaks allowed Behrman to form moral judgments in a great many plays, among them *Meteor, Amphitryon 38,* and *Jane;* but the mellow temperament prevented him from possessing an outright vindictiveness, even in a play like *Jacobowsky and the Colonel* where, with a certain comic detachment, he chose at the conclusion to look toward the dawning of a better era in human history that to treat the horrors of fascism with all of the vindictiveness he might have.

Behrman is the humane product of the same American Dream at which he had scoffed as a young man but which he came to embrace as a matured writer when what he wrote lent credence (as, for example, in *The Worcester Account*) to the fabled promise of America. Even then, however, Behrman looked at America with a critical but understanding point of view. In *Meteor*, for instance, Raphael Lord's dynamic urge to rise spectacularly in the capitalistic system results in a moral and economic catastrophe, not because the system itself is necessarily corrupt, but because Lord himself does not play within such rules as exist. The same general explanation can be applied to a play like *Dunnigan's Daughter* in which Clay Ranier's shabby sense of values is at fault, not his fundamental desire to become an economic "success." A reading of *Duveen* also illustrates that the American millionaires who were Duveen's customers are not unsophisticated because of their exposure to the American Dream but because they themselves are conspicuously and regrettably short on aesthetic and moral cultivation.

In real life Behrman developed this aesthetic and moral cultivation in himself. He played by ethical standards and wrote to the end that others might be pleasantly entertained while they were gently but seriously informed at the same time. In plays like *Biography*, *Rain from Heaven*, and *End of Summer* Behrman commented on the need for mutual toleration of social and political views; and he did so with an element of wittiness. In the first act of *End of Summer*, for example, a conversation between old Mrs. Wyler and the young radical Will Dexter is well in progress when she poses a question: "I suppose you're one of those young radicals our colleges are said to be full of nowadays. Tell me, what do you young radicals stand for?" Dexter replies with a comic, if honest, answer: "I haven't decided exactly what I'm for, but I'm pretty certain what I'm against." Such exchanges as these are serious in a comic vein, and they contain in essence the comic approach that endeared him to both critics and theater audiences. Throughout his career Behrman appealed to his public through the intellect and the heart, never through the glands. He believed quite realistically and without naiveté in the proposition that life can be savored and refined and that the human race can, if it wishes, be perfected and improved upon beyond anything commonly considered possible. He preferred to think of man as a fragment of God, as he wrote in *Rain from Heaven*, rather than as a highly developed animal. Most of all, he illustrated in his own life and writing that it is not only preferable but reasonable that human beings can laugh and yet come to terms with the stark reality of life.

Notes and References

Chapter One

1. *The Worcester Account* (New York, 1954), p. 16.
2. *Ibid.*, p. 188.
3. *Ibid.*, p. 74.
4. *Ibid.*, p. 209.
5. *Ibid.*, p. 98.
6. *Ibid.*, p. 219.
7. *Ibid.*, p. 210.
8. *Ibid.*
9. *The Suspended Drawing Room* (New York, 1965), p. 90.
10. Noted in Lewis Williams Heniford, "S. N. Behrman as a Social Dramatist" (Ph.D. dissertation, Stanford University, 1964), p. 21.
11. *The Clark College Monthly* III, no. 1 (October, 1913), p. 15.
12. *Ibid.*, III, no. 8 (May, 1914), p. 314.
13. *Celebrities at Our Hearthside* (Boston, 1959), p. 385.
14. "Harvard Class of 1916: 25th Anniversary Report" (1940), p. 41.
15. *Ibid.*, p. 40.
16. *Ibid.*
17. *Ibid.*, p. 41.
18. Maurice Zolotow, *Stagestruck* (New York, 1965), p. 163.
19. *The Worcester Account*, p. 238.
20. *The New York Times*, March 8, 1931, sec. VIII, p. 4.
21. "Writer Defends Producers," *The New York Times*, January 14, 1934, sec. IX, p. 5.
22. "In Defense of Hollywood," *The New Yorker*, January 20, 1934, p. 33.
23. "Five Playwrights Plus Brotherly Love," *The New York Times*, August 28, 1938, sec. IX, p. 2.

24. "Harvard Class of 1916: 25th Anniversary Report" (1940), p. 39.

25. "Hoppin Estate Sold," *The New York Times*, January 17, 1942, p. 26.

26. *Portrait of Max* (New York, 1960), p. 54.

Chapter Three

1. Maurice Zolotow, *Stagestruck*, p. 97.

2. *Ibid.*, p. 164.

3. "People in a Diary—II," *The New Yorker*, May 20, 1972, p. 39.

4. Langner, Lawrence, *The Magic Curtain* (New York, 1951), p. 219.

5. "People in a Diary—I," *The New Yorker*, May 13, 1972, p. 68.

6. "People in a Diary—II," *The New Yorker*, May 20, 1972, p. 62.

7. *Ibid.*, p. 40.

8. *Ibid.*, p. 86.

9. *The Nation*, January 9, 1935, p. 56.

10. *The Commonweal*, February 28, 1936, p. 497.

Chapter Four

1. "People in a Diary—II," *The New Yorker*, May 20, 1972, p. 39.

2. *Ibid.*, p. 42.

3. This unpublished translation is among the *Amphitryon 38* notes and papers which Behrman gave to the Wisconsin Center for Theater Research and which are currently shelved at the state historical society.

4. "People in a Diary—II," *The New Yorker*, May 20, 1972, p. 41.

5. George Freedly, *The Lunts* (London, Theatre World Monographs No. 10, 1957), p. 70.

6. *Stagestruck*, p. 222.

7. Joseph Wood Krutch, *The Nation*, April 29, 1939, p. 509.

8. Walcott Gibbs, *The New Yorker*, March 8, 1941, p. 34.

9. Brooks Atkinson, *The New York Times*, February 25, 1941.

10. *Stagestruck*, p. 234.

11. Lawrence Langner, *The Magic Curtain* (New York, E. P. Dutton and Company, Inc., 1951), p. 337.

12. *Ibid.*, p. 338.

13. "People in a Diary—II," *The New Yorker*, May 20, 1972, p. 39.

14. *The New York Times*, February 7, 1943, sec. 2, p. 2.

15. Joseph Wood Krutch, *The Nation*, December 12, 1942, p. 659.

16. Louis Kronenberger, *PM* (New York newspaper), November 26, 1942.

17. "People in a Diary—II," *The New Yorker*, May 20, 1972, p. 92.

18. Stark Young, *The New Republic*, March 27, 1944, p. 407.

19. Ward Morehouse, *The New York Sun*, December 27, 1945.

20. Richard Watts, Jr., *The New York Post*, November 3, 1949.

21. Ward Morehouse, *The New York Sun*, November 3, 1949.

22. Margaret Marshall, *The Nation,* November 19, 1949, p. 498.

23. Brooks Atkinson, *The New York Times,* November 3, 1949.

24. "People in a Diary—II," *The New Yorker,* May 20, 1972, p. 39.

25. *The Magic Curtain,* p. 426.

26. S.N. Behrman, *The New York Times,* March 30, 1952, sec. 2, p. 3.

27. Walter Kerr, *The New York Herald Tribune,* February 2, 1952.

28. *Ibid.,* December 9, 1958.

29. John Chapman, *The New York Daily News,* December 9, 1958.

30. Anon., *America,* January 10, 1959.

31. Richard Hayes, *The Commonweal,* February 6, 1959, p. 496.

32. John Chapman, *The New York Daily News,* November 20, 1962.

33. *Stagestruck,* p. 259.

34. Richard Watts, Jr., *The New York Post,* March 13, 1964.

35. John McCarten, *The New Yorker,* March 21, 1964, p. 64.

Chapter Five

1. October 24, 1954, p. 4

2. David Cecil, *Max* (Boston, 1965), p. 479.

3. "People in a Diary—I," *The New Yorker,* May 13, 1972, p. 87.

4. Ruth Gambee, *Library Journal,* November 15, 1968, p. 4305.

5. Granville Hicks, *The Saturday Review,* July 20, 1968, p. 22.

6. Anon., *Time,* August 2, 1968, p. 67.

7. Naomi Bliven, *The New Yorker,* December 7, 1968, p. 240.

8. "People in a Diary—I," p. 87.

Chapter Six

1. Lawrence Langner, *The Magic Curtain* (New York, 1951), p. 220.

2. S. N. Behrman, *The New York Times,* March 30, 1952, sec. II, pp. 1, 3.

Chapter Seven

1. Gerald Rabkin, *Drama and Commitment* (Bloomington, Indiana; 1964), p. 323.

2. "People in a Diary—I," *The New Yorker,* May 13, 1972, p. 44.

3. *Stagestruck,* p. 65.

4. In spite of their differences, Behrman seemed to have had a high regard for Moeller. He wrote in his memoirs: "I was lucky to find Phil Moeller; he suited me perfectly" ("People in a Diary—I," *The New Yorker,* May 13, 1972, p. 90).

5. *Stagestruck,* p. 166.

6. W. David Sievers, *Freud on Broadway* (New York, 1955), pp. 322, 336.

7. *Ibid.,* p. 323.

Chapter Eight

1. Joseph Wood Krutch, *The American Drama Since 1918* (New York, 1939), p. 181.

2. John Gassner, "S. N. Behrman: The Risk of Tolerance," *Theatre Arts*, May, 1952, p. 32.

3. *Ibid.*, p. 97.

Selected Bibliography

Aside from the major plays and the six volumes of prose, the early writings of S. N. Behrman are difficult to track down. He is said to have contributed a number of essays to popular and sometimes left-wing periodicals between about 1915 and 1926. The bibliographer who searches for them finds the going exceedingly difficult, for even Behrman himself had lost track of his early publications. Most of the early essays, however, are listed here, and the listing undoubtedly is ample enough for one to see the directions Behrman's mind was taking in that period of his life.

It should be understood also that the published editions of the plays are necessarily different in minor respects from the text of the play as performed on stage, since Behrman, his directors, and his actors were given to textual modification whenever it seemed advisable. The original Behrman manuscripts—along with an extensive quantity of letters, reviews, playbills and other materials—are deposited at The State Historical Society of Wisconsin in Madison. It should be added that, while many have commented about the writer and his writing, very few of their comments are worthy of being commended to a general audience. Only the more significant of secondary sources are listed below.

PRIMARY SOURCES

1. Published Plays (Listed chronologically in order of their production)
Bedside Manners. (with J. Kenyon Nicholson) New York: Samuel French, 1924.
A Night's Work. (with J. Kenyon Nicholson) New York: Samuel French, 1926.
The Second Man. New York: Samuel French, 1926.
Serena Blandish, or The Difficulty of Getting Married. Anthologized in *Three Plays: Serena Blandish, Meteor, The Second Man.* New York: Farrar and Rinehart, 1934.
Meteor. New York: Samuel French, 1934.
Brief Moment. New York: Farrar and Rinehart, 1931.
Biography. New York: Farrar and Rinehart, 1933.
Rain from Heaven. New York: Random House, 1934.

End of Summer. New York: Random House, 1936.
Amphitryon 38. New York: Random House, 1938.
Wine of Choice. New York: Random House, 1938.
No Time for Comedy. New York: Random House, 1939.
The Talley Method. New York: Random House, 1941.
The Pirate. New York: Random House, 1943.
Jacobowsky and the Colonel. New York: Random House, 1944.
Dunnigan's Daughter. New York: Random House, 1946.
I Know My Love. New York: Samuel French, 1949.
Jane. New York: Random House, 1952.
Fanny. New York: Random House. 1955.
The Cold Wind and the Warm. New York: Random House, 1959.
Lord Pengo. New York: Random House, 1963.
But For Whom Charlie. New York: Random House, 1964.

2.   Prose Works

Duveen. New York: Random House, 1952. Illustrated Edition: Boston: Lit-
   tle, Brown and Company, 1972.
The Worcester Account. New York, Random House, 1954.
Portrait of Max: An Intimate Memoir of Sir Max Beerbohm. New York:
   Random House, 1960.
The Suspended Drawing Room. New York: Stein and Day, 1965.
The Burning Glass. Boston: Little, Brown and Company, 1968.
People in a Diary. Boston: Little, Brown and Company, 1972.

3.   Miscellaneous Essays, Letters

"Park-Bench Lovers." *The Clark College Monthly* II, No. 3, (November,
   1912), 133–34.
"Culture and Shaves." *The Clark College Monthly* II, No. 5, (January,
   1913), 193.
"Via Music." *The Clark College Monthly* II, No. 5, (January, 1913), 223–25.
"The Man Who Hated." *The Clark College Monthly* II, No. 6, (February,
   1913), 283–88.
"Bought and Paid for." *The Clark College Monthly* III, No. 2, (November,
   1913), 94–96.
"Damaged Goods." *The Clark College Monthly* III, No. 3, (December,
   1913), 94–96.
"Caesar and Cleopatra." *The Clark College Monthly* III, No. 5, (February,
   1914), 193–94.
"The Destroyer." *The Clark College Monthly* III, No. 7, (April, 1914),
   256–68.
"Psychology and the New Philosophy of the Theatre." *The Clark College
   Monthly* III, No. 8, (May, 1914), 303–7.

"The Song of Ariel." *The Seven Arts*, May, 1917, pp. 13–26.

"Movie Morals." *The New Republic* XII (August 25, 1917), 100–1.

"The Coming of the Lord." *The Touchstone* II (October, 1917), 76–81.

"Surrender." *The Liberator*, May, 1918, pp. 16–18.

"Lord Morley as a Literary Critic." M.A. Thesis, Columbia University, 1918.

"The Return." *The Smart Set* LX (November, 1918), 113–19.

"Tawny Makes a Visit." *The Smart Set* LVIII (March, 1919), 67–73.

"Honorary Pall-Bearers Were—." *The Smart Set* LX (April, 1919), 121–26.

"Rupert Hughes and Karl Marx." *The New Republic* XIX (July 9, 1919), 335–36.

"That Second Man." *The Smart Set* LX (November, 1919), 73–84.

"The Advertising Man." *The New Republic* XX (August 20, 1919), 84–86.

"Iron." *The New Republic* XX (August 20, 1919), 100–1.

"Hickey and Mother Goose." *The Liberator* III (March, 1920), 11–13.

"Never Stretch Your Legs in a Taxi." *The Smart Set* LXII (August, 1920), 71–76.

"The Wraith." *The Smart Set* LXII (November, 1920), 91–95.

"Rupert Goes on the Loose" (with J. Kenyon Nicholson). *The Smart Set* LXVII (March, 1922), 53–58.

"Holiday" (with J. Kenyon Nicholson). The Smart Set LXVIII (June, 1922), 89–96.

"Piano" (with J. Kenyon Nicholson). *The Smart Set* LXVIII (August, 1922), 25–30.

"En Route." *The Smart Set* LXIX (November, 1922), 127–30.

"The Bathroom Key" (with J. Kenyon Nicholson). *The Smart Set* LXX (April, 1923), 75–83.

"Loan Exhibit" (with J. Kenyon Nicholson). *The Smart Set* LXXI (June, 1923), 119–28.

"Troubadour." *The New Yorker* V (May 25, 1929), 27–29.

"Accoucheur." *The New Yorker* VIII (February 6, 1932), 20–24.

"Mr. Jaeckel and a Few Hides." *The New Yorker* VIII (April 9, 1932), 22–25.

"Chutspo." *The New Yorker* VIII (December 10, 1932), 23–27.

"In Defense of Hollywood." *The New Yorker* IX (January 20, 1934), 30–35.

"Do or Diaphragm." *The New Yorker* XI (May 25, 1935), 22–27.

"Hyper or Hypo?" *The New Yorker* XV (April 8, 1939), 23–29.

"Old Monotonous." *The New Yorker* XVI (June 1, 1940), 33–36.

"Old Monotonous." *The New Yorker* XVI (June 8, 1940), 23–26.

"Zion Comes to Culver City." In *Chaim Weizman*, ed. M. W. Weisgal. New York: Dial Press, 1944.

"The Suspended Drawing Rooom." *The New Yorker* XX (January 27, 1945), 27–32.

"The Red and the Blue." *The New Yorker* XXI (April 21, 1945), 30–34.

"Playwright." *The New Yorker* XXII (May 25, 1946), 28–34.

"Playwright." *The New Yorker* XXII (June 1, 1946), 32–36, 39–40, 42–46.

"Playwright." *The New Yorker* XXII (June 8, 1946), 32–38.

"Mr. Lavin, Mr. Lupkin and Dr. Abercrombie." *The New Yorker* XXII (June 29, 1946), 28–30, 33.

"Our Responsive Readers." *The New Yorker* XXII (August 3, 1946), 63–65.

"My Romance With Eleonora Sears." *The New Yorker* XXII (January 18, 1947), 28–30.

"It's Cold at Lady Windermere's." *The New Yorker* XXIII (March 22, 1947), 37–42.

"Mr. Wolfson's Stained-Glass Window." *The New Yorker* XXIII (June 28, 1947), 24–28.

"Debs and the Day of Atonement." *The New Yorker* XXIII (December 6, 1947), 42–45.

"Reporter at Large." *The New Yorker* XXIII (March 22, 1947), 37–42.

"The Improvement in Mr. Gaynor's Technique." *The New Yorker* XXIV (July 17, 1948), 25–29.

"Notes of a Popular Pessimist." *The New Yorker* XXV (October 29, 1949), 102–4, 107–9.

"The Days of Duveen: Itinerary." *The New Yorker* XXVII (September 29, 1951), 33–38.

"The Days of Duveen: A Beginning in Delft." *The New Yorker* XXVII (October 6, 1951), 41–44.

"The Days of Duveen, A Brisk Market in Immortality." *The New Yorker* XXVII (October 13, 1951), 41–46.

"The Days of Duveen: B.B." *The New Yorker* XXVII (October 20, 1951), 36–40.

"The Days of Duveen: The Blue Boy and Two Lavinias." *The New Yorker* XXVII (October 27, 1951), 38–40.

"The Days of Duveen: The Silent Men." *The New Yorker* XXVII (November 3, 1951), 40–42.

"Malach Hamovis." *The New Yorker* XXVII (January 26, 1952), 21–29.

"Raising a Query: What Makes Comedy High?" *The New York Times*, March 30, 1952, sec. II, pp. 1, 3.

"Daughter of the Ramaz." *The New Yorker* XXIX (November 1, 1953), 45–52.

"Double Chocolate with Emma and Sasha." *The New Yorker* XXIX (January 16, 1954), 24–29.

"A Little Glass of Warmth." *The New Yorker* XXX (May 1, 1954), 28–36.

"The Point of the Needle." *The New Yorker* XXX (June 5, 1954), 26–34.

"Books." *The New Yorker* XXXI (October 29, 1955), 154–56.

"The History of the Russian Revolution." *The New Yorker* XXXII (November 24, 1956), 47–51.

"Books." *The New Yorker* XXXII (January 26, 1957), 103–5.

"Conversation With Max: Compare Me." *The New Yorker* XXXV (February 6, 1960), 45–46.

"Conversation With Max: The Mirror." *The New Yorker* XXXV (February 13, 1960), 40–42.

"Conversation With Max: On the Terrace." *The New Yorker* XXXVI (February 20, 1960), 50–52.

"Conversation With Max: Partito Ma Non Arrivato." *The New Yorker* XXXVI (February 27, 1960), 43–44.

"Conversation With Max: The Menu." *The New Yorker* XXXVI (March 12, 1960), 47–48.

"Conversation With Max: The Executive Forefinger." *The New Yorker* XXXVI (March 12, 1960), 50–52.

"The Paddy Vein." *Prairie Schooner* XXXV (Spring, 1961), 10–13.

"Letter to the Editor." *The New York Times,* June 14, 1963, p. 30.

"You Can't Release Dante's Inferno in the Summertime." *The New York Times Magazine,* July 17, 1966, pp. 6–7.

"Speaking as a Survivor, Not a Contemporary." *The New York Times Magazine,* June 2, 1968, pp. 28–29.

"People in a Diary—I." *The New Yorker* XLVIII (May 13, 1972), 36–94.

"People in a Diary—II." *The New Yorker* XLVIII (May 20, 1972), 39–95.

"People in a Diary—III." *The New Yorker* XLVIII (May 27, 1972), 38–81.

SECONDARY SOURCES

ASHER, DONALD. *The Eminent Yachtsman and the Whorehouse Piano Player.* New York: Coward, McCann & Geohegan, 1973. Concerns the friendship of S. N. Behrman and Daniel Asher. Written by Asher's son.

DODD, LORING HOLMES. *Celebrities at Our Hearthside.* Boston: Chapman and Grimes, 1955. Warm remembrance of Behrman as an undergraduate at Clark College as recalled by one of his professors.

GASSNER, JOHN. "S. N. Behrman: The Risk of Tolerance" *The American Theatre as Seen by Its Critics.* Ed. by M. J. Moses and J. M. Brown. New York: W. W. Norton and Co., 1934. Shrewd, incisive look at the artistic and ideological bases of Behrman's early plays.

HENIFORD, LEWIS WILLIAMS "S. N. Behrman as a Social Dramatist. Ph.D. dissertation, Stanford University, 1964. Resourceful, reasonably comprehensive view of the Behrman biography, the major plays, and prose pieces. Assembles most of what was said and known about Behrman and his work up to 1964.

KAPLAN, CHARLES. "S. N. Behrman: The Quandary of the Comic Spirit." *College English* XI (March, 1950), 317–23. Deals with some of the major thematic strains in the plays; speculates on Behrman's response as a comic writer to the tragedy of his time.

KRUTCH, JOSEPH WOOD. *The American Drama Since 1918: An Informal*

History. New York: Random House, 1939. Admiring, fairly comprehensive treatment of the plays concluding with *No Time for Comedy.* Identifies the thematic direction of Behrman's comedies before 1940.

LEVIN, MILTON I. "S. N. Behrman: The Operation and Dilemmas of the Comic Spirit." Ph.D. dissertation, University of Michigan, 1958. Examination of "the dramatic work of Behrman in its historical context" with attention to Behrman's relationship to the general comic philosophy and forms which have developed since the late nineteenth century, and the specific fluctuations in the intellectual climate between 1925 and 1955. . . ."

MANTLE, BURNS. *Contemporary American Playwrights.* New York: Dodd, Mead and Co., 1938. Early, rather sketchy but affirmative assessment of Behrman as seen from the late 1930s.

QUINN, ARTHUR H. *A History of the American Drama from the Civil War to the Present Day.* Vol. II. Revised ed. New York: F. S. Crofts and Co., 1936. Significant, valuable judgment of Behrman in the context of American theater history and of his time.

SIEVERS, DAVID W. *Freud on Broadway.* New York: Hermitage House, 1953. Mistakenly identifies Behrman closely with "the post-Freudian playwrights of the thirties."

Index